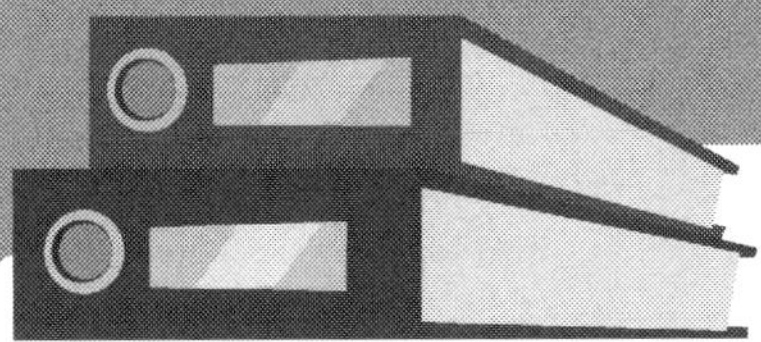

Science

Daily Practice Workbook

20 weeks of fun activities

ARGOPREP

Physical Science • Life Science • Earth & Space Science • Engineering

ArgoPrep is one of the leading providers of supplemental educational products and services. We offer affordable and effective test prep solutions to educators, parents and students. Learning should be fun and easy! To access more resources visit us at www.argoprep.com.

Our goal is to make your life easier, so let us know how we can help you by e-mailing us at: info@argoprep.com.

- ArgoPrep is a recipient of the prestigious **Mom's Choice Award**.
- ArgoPrep also received the 2019 **Seal of Approval** from Homeschool.com for our award-winning workbooks.
- ArgoPrep was awarded the 2019 **National Parenting Products Award**, **Gold Medal Parent's Choice Award** and **the Tillywig Brain Child Award.**

ISBN: 9781951048464

Published by Argo Brothers.

SCIENCE SERIES

Science Daily Practice Workbook by ArgoPrep is an award-winning series created by certified science teachers to help build mastery of foundational science skills. Our workbooks explore science topics in depth with ArgoPrep's 5 E'S to build science mastery: Engaging, Exploring, Explaining, Experimenting, and Elaborating. All of our curriculum is aligned with the latest Next Generation Science Standards.

BOOKS BY ARGOPREP

Here are some other test prep workbooks by ArgoPrep you may be interested in. All of our workbooks come equipped with detailed video explanations to make your learning experience a breeze! Visit us at www.argoprep.com

COMMON CORE MATH SERIES

COMMON CORE ELA SERIES

COMMON CORE TEST SERIES

The goal of these workbooks is to provide mock state tests so students can increase confidence and test scores during actual test day.

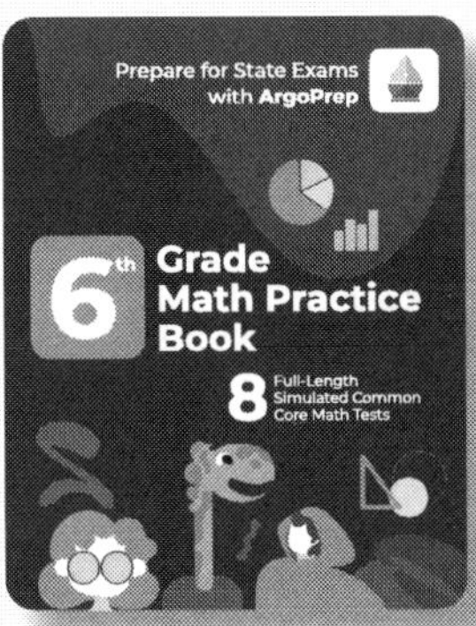

INTRODUCING MATH!

Introducing Math! by ArgoPrep is an award-winning series created by certified teachers to provide students with high-quality practice problems. Our workbooks include topic overviews with instruction, practice questions, answer explanations along with digital access to video explanations. Practice in confidence - with ArgoPrep!

KIDS SUMMER ACADEMY SERIES

ArgoPrep's Kids Summer Academy series helps prevent summer learning loss and gets students ready for their new school year by reinforcing core foundations in math, english and science. Our workbooks also introduce new concepts so students can get a head start and be on top of their game for the new school year!

SUMMER ACTIVITY PLAYGROUND SERIES

Summer Activity Playground is another summer series that is designed to prevent summer learning loss and prepares students for the new school year. Students will be able to practice math, ELA, science, social studies and more! This is a new released series that offers the latest aligned learning standards for each grade.

Take a look inside

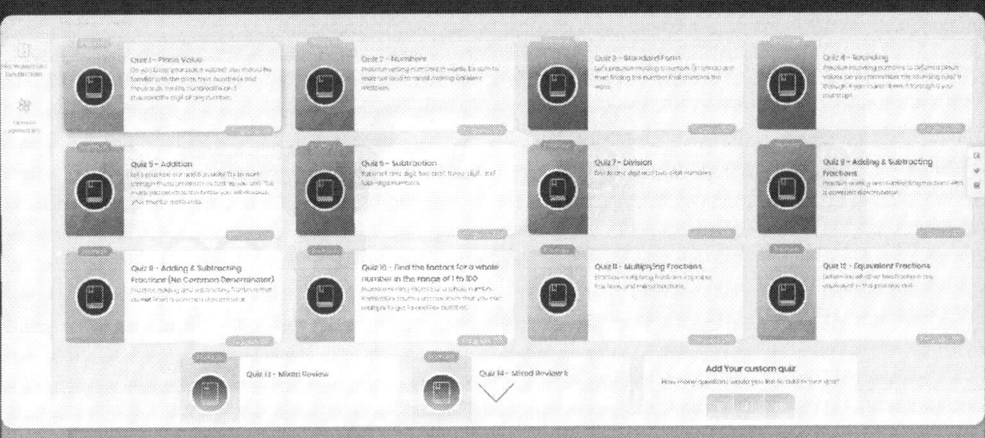

Testimonials

Read all testimonails

I love these books, both the multiple choice and the free response. They are quite challenging math problems that really require critical thinking, and a true understanding of the relationship between numbers. I am a homeschooling parent, and have used these books for 3rd grade and now 4th grade math. These books provide excellent practice especially in word problems across all topic areas.

Samanta K.
1 month ago

Awesome practice to brainstorm your kids' math knowledge; keeps my son's attention and interest to work with this book!!! He loves it! Definitely a good buy!

Olga Kuznec
2 month ago

Your annual subscription includes **two free** workbooks shipped **directly to your home**.

Kindergarten 1st grade 2nd grade 3rd grade 4th grade 5th grade 6th grade 7th grade 8th grade

Subscribe for 12 months and get 2 workbooks **for free**

$ 119.88 ~~199.88$~~ save 40%

SUBSCRIBE

 Child Safe Parent Monitoring  No Ads  No External Links

Table of Contents

Introduction

Welcome to our 8th grade science workbook!

This workbook has been specifically designed to help students build mastery of foundational science skills that are taught in 8th grade. Included are 20 weeks of comprehensive instruction, working through the four branches of science: Physical Science, Life Science, Earth & Space Science and Engineering. This workbook dedicates five weeks of instruction to each of the four branches of science, focusing on different standards within each week of instruction. Within the branch of Physical Science, students will learn about thermal energy and the law of conservation. In Life Science, they will learn more about ecosystems and populations as well as the importance of biodiversity. Earth & space science explores climate change and human impact on resources. Finally, in the Engineering section, students will be able to clearly identify a problem, create a solution and test their ideas. At the conclusion of the 20 weeks of instruction, students should have a solid grasp on the concepts required of the Next Generation Science Standards for 8th grade.

How to Use the Book

All 20 weeks of daily activity pages in this book follow the same weekly structure. The book is divided into four sections: Physical Science, Life Science, Earth & Space Science and Engineering. The activities in each of the sections align to the Next Generation Science Standards which will help prepare students for state standardized assessments. While the sections can be completed in any order, it is important to complete each week within the section in chronological order, as the skills often build upon one another. Each week focuses on one specific topic within the section. More information about the weekly structure can be found in the Weekly Planner section.

Weekly Planner

Day	Activity	Description
1	Engaging with the Topic	Read a short text on the topic and answer multiple choice questions.
2	Exploring the Topic	Interact with the topic on a deeper level by collecting, analyzing and interpreting data.
3	Explaining the Topic	Make sense of the topic by explaining and beginning to draw conclusions about the data.
4	Experimenting with the Topic	Investigate the topic through hands-on, easy to implement experiments.
5	Elaborating on the Topic	Reflect on the topic and use all information learned to draw conclusions and evaluate results.

How to watch video explantions

Download our app:
ArgoPrep Video Explanations
to access videos on any mobile device or tablet.

or you can access it on our website:

Step 1 - Visit our website at: www.argoprep.com/k8

Step 2 - Click on the"Video Explanations button located on the top right corner.

Step 3 - Choose the workbook you have and enjoy video explanations.

List of Topics

Unit	Week	Topic	Standard
Physical Science	1	Synthetic Materials	MS-PS1-3
Physical Science	2	Thermal Energy	MS-PS1-4
Physical Science	3	Law Of Conservation	MS-PS1-5
Physical Science	4	Newton's 3rd Law	MS-PS2-1
Physical Science	5	Waves	MS-PS4-2
Life Science	6	Physiology	MS-LS1-8
Life Science	7	Ecosystems & Populations	MS-LS2-4
Life Science	8	Biodiversity	MS-LS2-5
Life Science	9	Modeling Evolution	MS-LS4-6
Life Science	10	Genetic Modification	MS-LS4-5
Earth & Space Science	11	Scaling The Solar System	MS-ESS1-3
Earth & Space Science	12	Changes In Earth's Surface Over Time	MS-ESS2-2
Earth & Space Science	13	Cycling Of Water On Earth	MS-ESS2-4
Earth & Space Science	14	Climate Change	MS-ESS3-5
Earth & Space Science	15	Human Impact On Resources	MS-ESS3-4
Engineering	16	Identifying The Problem	MS-ETS1-1
Engineering	17	Creating a Solution	MS-ETS1-2
Engineering	18	Testing Ideas	MS-ETS1-4
Engineering	19	Analyzing Test Results	MS-ETS1-3
Engineering	20	Editing Ideas & Designs	MS-ETS1-4

Next Generation Science Standards Correlation Guide

Unit	Week	Next Generation Science Standard	Description of Standard
Physical Science	1	MS-PS1-3	Compare and contrast the different types of natural and synthetic fabrics.
Physical Science	2	MS-PS1-4	Plan and conduct an investigation to determine how thermal energy impacts particle motion in various household liquids.
Physical Science	3	MS-PS1-5	Make observations to construct an evidence-based account about the conservation of mass with various chemical equations.
Physical Science	4	MS-PS2-1	Use observations to explain how birds can use Newton's Third Law to fly.
Physical Science	5	MS-PS4-2	Make observations to construct an evidence-based account about how waves of light can reflect and move through objects.
Life Science	6	MS-LS1-8	Make observations to construct an evidence-based account about how the nervous system functions.
Life Science	7	MS-LS2-4	Read texts and use media to explore how keystone species' populations affect ecosystems.
Life Science	8	MS-LS4-5	Read texts and use media to determine the need to protect biodiversity both for ethical and other reasons.
Life Science	9	MS-LS4-6	Make observations and gather information about how different populations of organisms evolve to best fit their environment.
Life Science	10	MS-LS2-5	Read texts and use media to explore how bioengineering is changing the agriculture, namely GMOs

Unit	Week	Next Generation Science Standard	Description of Standard
Earth & Space Science	11	MS-ESS1-3	Use tools and materials to design and build a scale model of our Solar System..
Earth & Space Science	12	MS-ESS2-2	Use observations of local geography and research other biomes to explore how geoscientific processes have changed Earth's surface over time.
Earth & Space Science	13	MS-ESS2-4	Use tools and materials to design a model of how water cycles on Earth.
Earth & Space Science	14	MS-ESS3-5	Make observations and analyze data/ articles to determine how global temperatures have changed over time and that effect on other aspects of the environment.
Earth & Space Science	15	MS-ESS3-4	Read texts and use media to compare how populations of three different countries differ and how it impacts resource usage.
Engineering	16	MS-ETS1-1	Make observations about a product or problem which could be improved through the use of scientific principles.
Engineering	17	MS-ETS1-2	Develop a model or an illustration that proposes a solution to the product or problem, clearly defining how its form relates to its function.
Engineering	18	MS-ETS1-4	Develop a step-by-step process to test your model/idea and gather quantitative data about its effectiveness.
Engineering	19	MS-ETS1-3	Analyze the data from testing and determine how it can be used to improve upon the original design idea.
Engineering	20	MS-ETS1-4	Re-design original idea and expand on the idea that editing ideas is an important part of the process.

WEEK 1

Physical Science

Synthetic Materials

MS-PS1-3

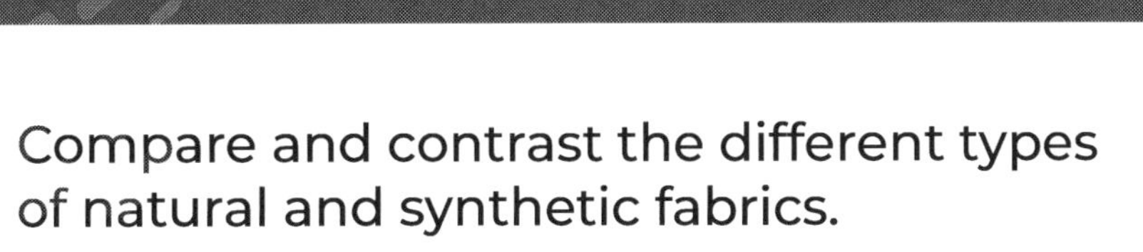

Week 1 Synthetic Materials

Day 1 ENGAGING WITH THE TOPIC

Directions: Read the text below. Then answer the questions that follow.

What Are Synthetic Materials?

Many materials we use on a daily basis are **natural** or **non-synthetic.** These are materials found in nature that have not been created by humans. Let's consider fabric for a moment. Fabrics such as cotton and wool are considered natural. Cotton comes directly from a plant and wool is grown by an animal. Even though these are processed by humans in order to weave fabric, they are not created by humans initially.

Synthetic materials, on the other hand, are created by humans. Many synthetic materials are made in labs through the combination of different **chemicals.** Let us think about fabric once more. Fabrics such as polyester, nylon and polyester are created through chemical reactions and have properties that humans want in a fabric such as the ability to stretch or not wrinkle.

1. Natural materials are:
   note: more than one answer may be correct for this question.

   A. Grown by plants
   B. Grown by animals
   C. Created in labs by humans
   D. All of the above

2. Synthetic materials are created through the process of:

   A. Farming
   B. Fabric making
   C. Chemical reactions
   D. None of the above

3. An example of a synthetic fabric is ....

   A. Cotton
   B. Nylon
   C. Wool
   D. Wood

Synthetic Materials

EXPLORING THE TOPIC

Yesterday, you learned the difference between natural and synthetic materials as well as how they are created. Today, you will explore these two types of materials.

Directions: Read each text below and complete the activity. Then answer the question that follows.

Looking At Materials Around You

Collect 10 different garments from your closet. Look at the tags on them and determine what type(s) of fabric they are made of. Write down each type of fabric you find and put a check mark next to the type each time you see a tag with that type of fabric listed.

1. What type of fabric was most common within your garments?

Exploring Natural Fabrics

Take a piece of cotton fabric (a 100% cotton t-shirt, napkin, etc) and wash it gently in your sink. Crumple it into a ball and put it on a table to dry overnight. Observe it in the morning.

2. When you washed the cotton fabric, did it absorb water easily?

   A. Yes **B.** No

3. When you lay out the fabric flat, after it dries overnight does it have wrinkles?

   A. Yes **B.** No

Exploring Synthetic Fabrics

Take a piece of polyester fabric (a 100% polyester garment, headband, etc) and wash it gently in your sink. Crumple it into a ball and put it on a table to dry overnight. Observe it in the morning.

4. When you washed the polyester fabric, did it absorb water easily?

   A. Yes **B.** No

5. When you lay out the fabric flat, after it dries overnight does it have wrinkles?

   A. Yes

   B. No

Yesterday, you explored the difference between natural and synthetic fibers found around the house. Today you will explain what you observed during those demonstrations.

Directions: Read each text below. Then answer the questions that follow.

Looking At Materials Around You

You discovered that garments are made from different types of fabrics, both natural and synthetic.

1. Explain why you think the most common type of fabric you found is used in garments. Describe its qualities: is it thick or thin? Durable or easy to tear? Was this fabric type dyed? It dyed more than one color or not?

Exploring Natural Fabrics

You discovered that cotton is absorbent and wrinkles easily.

2. Explain why cotton might be good for some products but not others.

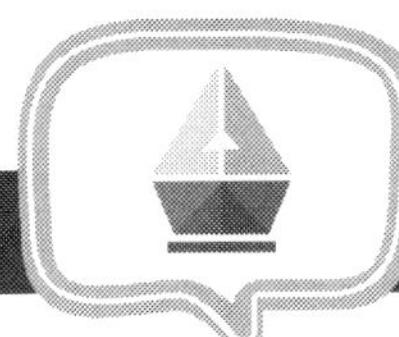

Exploring Synthetic Fabrics

You discovered that polyester is not absorbent and does not wrinkle easily.

3. Explain why polyester might be good for some products but not others.

You have spent several days learning about, exploring and explaining the difference between synthetic and natural materials.

Materials:

1. 12"X12" Squares of 4-6 fabric types, making sure you have both synthetic and natural fabric
   - **A.** Example of natural fabric: Silk, cotton, wool, linen, jute
   - **B.** Examples of synthetic fabric: Polyester, rayon, spandex, acrylic, microfiber cloth

   *You can either purchase these at a craft store or cut them from old, unwanted materials around you house - ask your parent first
2. Water
3. Dye, markers and/or paint

Procedure:

1. Cut your squares of each fabric type into 3"x3" pieces
2. Next, conduct the following experiments - make sure to record your observations so you can answer the questions below:
   - **A.** Experiment #1: Take a piece of each fabric and place it in water and observe how much water it absorbs as well as how much heavier it feels.
   - **B.** Experiment #2: Try to tear the fabric with your hands. Record if it tears and how hard it was to tear it.
   - **C.** Experiment #3: Try to stretch the fabric. Record if it stretches or not.
   - **D.** Experiment #4: Place paint or marker on each piece of fabric and let it sit for 10 minutes. Then rinse it in water and record if there is still pigment left of the fabric.

Follow-Up Questions:

1. What fabric was most absorbent? Was it natural or synthetic?

2. What fabric was easiest to tear? Was it natural or synthetic?

3. What fabric was stretchiest? Was it natural or synthetic?

4. What fabric was easiest to stain with either paint or marker? Was it natural or synthetic?

Synthetic Materials

ELABORATING ON THE TOPIC

Yesterday, you collected data while experimenting with synthetic and natural fabrics. You determined some of the properties of these types of materials. Today, you will use that data to draw conclusions about the difference between natural and synthetic fabrics.

Directions: Read and answer each question below.

1. What are some properties that natural fabrics all seem to share?

2. What are some properties that synthetic fabrics all seem to share?

3. Go online and research what other properties natural and synthetic fabrics tend to have. List two properties for each fabric type below.

4. Why do you think humans created synthetic fabrics so that they would have these qualities?

5. Pretend you are designing a sports jersey for your favorite team. What type of fabric would you want to use and why?

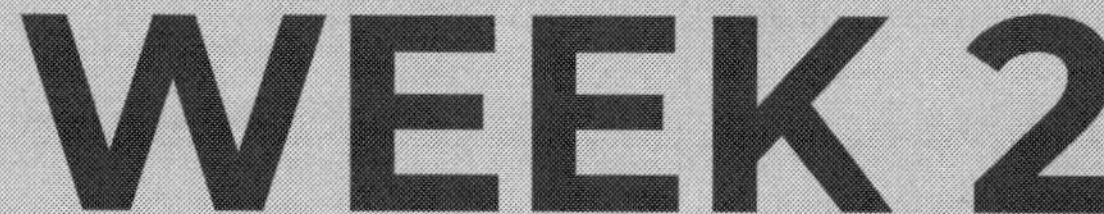

Physical Science

Thermal Energy

MS-PS1-4

Plan and conduct an investigation to determine how thermal energy impacts particle motion in various household liquids.

Week 2 Thermal Energy

Day 1 ENGAGING WITH THE TOPIC

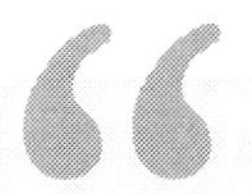

Directions: Read the text below. Then answer the questions that follow.

What Is Energy?

When we talk about **energy** in science, we define it as the ability to do work. This work can come in many different forms but it needs to be able to be transferred from one thing to another. For example, when you pick up a cup of tea, your body is doing work because the movement is being transferred from your arm to the cup.

There are two main forms of energy which include kinetic energy and potential energy. **Kinetic energy** depends on the movement of atoms and molecules. **Potential energy** depends on the amount of energy stored between the bonds of atoms. This week we are going to focus on a specific type of energy known as thermal energy.

Thermal energy is more commonly known as heat. The more thermal energy something has, the more its atoms are moving. The movement of the atoms is what is creating that heat.

1. Energy is define as the ability to do ______:

   A. Kinetics

   B. Transfers

   C. Work

   D. Storage

2. Kinetic energy is dependent on the ______ of atoms and molecules.

   A. Potential

   B. Heat

   C. Movement

   D. All of the above

3. What is another name for thermal energy?

   A. Work

   B. Potential

   C. Atomic energy

   D. Heat

Yesterday, you learned about energy and focused on the definition of thermal energy, also known as heat. Today you will explore some properties about thermal energy.

Directions: Read each text below and complete the activity. Then answer the question that follows.

Considering States Of Matter

Water is a pure substance, meaning it is only made of one molecule. If you place it in a freezer in an ice cube tray, it becomes solid. If you take it out of the freezer and put it on a plate, letting it be heated up to room temperature, it melts into liquid water. Water is free to move around on that plate now.

1. Which molecules of water are moving more, the ones in the ice or in the liquid water?

   A. Ice

   B. Water

Observing Movement In Water

Fill two identical glasses with the same amount of cold tap water. Place one in the microwave for 45-60 seconds and leave the other as is. Place them a few inches away from each other and without touching or stirring them, add two drops of food coloring to each at the same time. Observe the movement of the food coloring for a few minutes.

2. What do you notice about the food coloring in the hot cup of water?

Exploring Heat And Insulation

Find two identical cups and wrap one of them a few layers of aluminum foil. Boil water and pour equal amounts into both cups. Leave them for ten minutes and then come back and measure each cup's temperature with a kitchen thermometer.

3. Is there a difference in temperature of the water in the two cups after ten minutes?

Yesterday, you explored thermal energy in the pure substance of water. Today you will explain what happened during those demonstrations and how it relates to your understanding of energy.

Directions: Read each text below. Then answer the questions that follow.

Considering States Of Matter

You discovered that a pure substance can be in different states, namely solid or liquid, depending on how much thermal energy is in its environment.

1. Explain why you think liquid water's molecules are moving faster. What evidence do you have of that?

2. If we boiled the water and it turned into steam, what would that tell you about thermal energy and the state of gas?

Observing Movement In Water

You discovered that food coloring moved around and mixed into the hot cup of water faster.

3. As you add thermal energy or heat to water, what happens to the molecules?

Exploring Heat And Insulation

You discovered that a cup wrapped in aluminum will cause water to stay warmer than the same cup not wrapped in aluminum.

4. Explain how aluminum might impact the cooling of water in a cup.

You have spent several days learning about, exploring and explaining thermal energy. Today you will complete an experiment that further allows you to explore how thermal energy and insulation are related. You will use a freezer to remove thermal energy from water.

Materials:

1. 4 identical plastic cups
2. Water
3. Materials to insulate wrap around 3 of the cups. Materials can include thinner corrugated cardboard, felt, face cloths, newspaper, or bubble wrap.
4. Kitchen thermometer

Procedure:

1. Wrap the outside of three of the cups with three different materials of your choice.
2. Heat water until it is very hot but not boiling. Take the temperature of the water right before completing the next step.
3. Pour equal amounts of water into each of the four glass cups and place in your freezer. Make sure to place a piece of each different material over the top of each of the cups you insulated.
4. Wait between 30 minutes and one hour and then take all of the cups out - wait until you see some ice forming in at least some of the cups. Record what you see in terms of the state of the water. Also take the temperature of each cup of water.

Follow-Up Questions:

1. Were there any cups that had any amount of ice in them when you took them out of the freezer?

....

....

2. What happened to the water in the cup that was not insulated at all?

....

....

3. Which material was associated with the cup that had the least amount of ice in it?

4. What cup had the lowest temperature?

5. What cup had the highest temperature?

Yesterday, you collected data while experimenting with insulating materials and water. You determined some of the properties of these types of materials. Today, you will use that data to draw conclusions about how insulation and thermal energy relate to states of matter in pure substances.

Directions: Read and answer each question below.

1. What happened to the water molecules that had turned into ice in any of the glasses?

2. What is the relationship between insulating materials and thermal energy?

3. When water is insulated, what is happening with the movement of the molecules of water?

4. If I remove insulation from a cup that is in a freezer, what will happen to the state of matter of the water? Why?

5. If you were designing a lunch box, what types of materials would you want to consider using?

WEEK 3

Physical Science

Law Of Conservation

MS-PS1-5

$C_3H_8 + 5O_2 \rightarrow 4H_2O + 3CO_2 + heat$

$\ldots_4 + 2O_2 \rightarrow CO_2 + 2H_2O$

Make observations to construct an evidence-based account about the conservation of mass with various chemical equations.

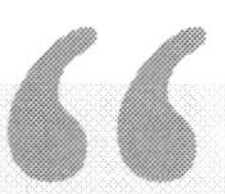

Directions: Read the text below. Then answer the questions that follow.

What Is The Law Of Conservation Of Mass?

In 1789 Antoine Lavoisier came up with the theory that matter can never be created nor destroyed during a chemical reaction. This became known as the **Law Of Conservation Of Mass.** The word "conservation" in physical science means constant or unchanging. Chemical reactions can rearrange atoms into different types of matter, but the total number of atoms remains the same before the reaction and after the reaction.

$$C_3H_8 + 5O_2 \rightarrow 4H_2O + 3CO_2 + \text{heat}$$

Consider the chemical equation above. This equation shows the chemical reaction that occurs when you burn propane gas in a grill. You create thermal energy (heat) as well as the byproducts of water (H_2O) and carbon dioxide (CO_2). If you were to count up the total number of carbons, hydrogens and oxygens on the left side of the equation and the total number of carbons, hydrogens and oxygens on the right side of the equation, you'd find the exact same number. Thanks to the Law Of Conservation Of Mass, the atoms are never destroyed, they are just rearranged into new things.

1. What does the word conservation mean in this context?

   A. Unstable
   B. Unchanged
   C. Total
   D. Reaction

2. During a chemical reaction, atoms can be:

   A. Created
   B. Destroyed
   C. Rearranged
   D. All of the above

3. When I burn propane (see example above), how much oxygen am I left with in the byproducts?.

   A. More than you started with
   B. Less than you started with
   C. The same amount that you started with
   D. There is not enough information to answer the question

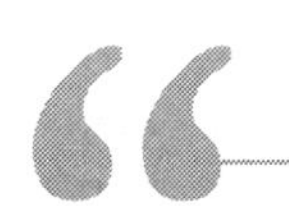

Yesterday, you learned about the Law Of Conservation Of Mass. Today we will explore this topic through demonstrations you conduct at home.

Directions: Read each text below and complete the activity. Then answer the question that follows.

Dissolving Sugar

Weigh 1 ounce of sugar. Pour 1 cup of water into a glass and weigh the whole glass. Add the weight of the sugar to the weight of the glass and write it down. Now mix the sugar into the water and stir it until it dissolves completely. Now weigh the glass of sugar water and record the weight.

1. Does the total weight of the water, glass and sugar added together change after the sugar is dissolved into the water?

Popcorn Before And After The Microwave

Get a bag of microwave popcorn and weigh it, bag and all, and record the weight. Pop the popcorn according to the manufacturer's directions in the microwave. As soon as it's done, place the bag unopened on the kitchen scale and weigh it once more.

2. Did the weight of the popcorn change after it was popped?

Mass Before & After A Reaction

Find a large plastic soda bottle with a screw-on cap and weigh it on a kitchen scale. Then weigh out 1 ounce of vinegar and 1 ounce of baking soda. Add those three weights together and write them down. Push some of the air out of the bottle and then quickly add the vinegar and baking soda into it using a funnel and close the top. After the reaction has taken place, weigh the bottle without dumping anything out.

3. What did you notice about the weight of the ingredients and the bottle before the reaction took place compared with after the reaction took place?

Yesterday, you explored the Law Of Conservation Of Mass through demonstrations of simple chemical reactions. Today you will consider your findings and explain what you observed.

Directions: Read each text below. Then answer the questions that follow.

Dissolving Sugar

You discovered that when sugar is dissolved in a glass of water, the total weight of all of those components does not change. Dissolving is a physical change of the sugar (the crystals get smaller and smaller until we cannot see them) but it is not a chemical change such as a chemical reaction like caramelizing sugar in a pan.

1. Why doesn't the weight change after you have dissolved the sugar?

Popcorn Before And After The Microwave

You discovered that the weight of popcorn does not change after you microwave it.

2. What does this tell you about the reaction that occurs in order to pop popcorn as it relates to the Law Of Conservation Of Mass?

Mass Before & After A Reaction

You discovered that after baking soda and vinegar react in a closed environment (i.e. a plastic soda bottle) the overall mass of all of the substances today does not change.

3. Even though this is a vigorous reaction with a lot of change you can see, what does this demonstrate about the Law Of Conservation Of Mass?

Law Of Conservation Of Mass

EXPERIMENTING WITH THE TOPIC

You have spent several days learning about, exploring and explaining the Law Of Conservation Of Mass. Today you will further explore this topic through the chemical reaction of combustion.

Think About This...

You are going camping and decide you want to put the Law Of Conservation into practice. You weigh your wood for your campfire and then find a way to weigh the weight of the fire (or energy) produced. You are also able to determine the weight of the smoke (Yes! Smoke has a weight) and the ashes.

Follow-Up Questions:

1. What is the name of this chemical reaction?

....

....

....

....

2. Where is most of the weight before the chemical reaction takes place?

....

....

....

....

3. Where is most of the weight after the chemical reaction takes place?

....

....

....

4. What is true of both of the materials you answered with in questions #2 and #3?

5. What do you notice about the sum of the weight of the log and the fire compared with the sum of the weight of the ashes and the smoke?

6. If you increased the amount of wood you burned, what would happen to the final weight of your two products of ashes and smoke?

Law Of Conservation Of Mass

ELABORATING ON THE TOPIC

Yesterday, you considered the reaction of combustion and determined how it showed how the Law Of Conservation Of Mass works. Today you will elaborate on that work and expand on it.

Directions: Read and answer each question below.

1. When you burn something, are the atoms in what you burn destroyed?

2. Do only solid things have weight?

3. If I did not have the same weight on one side of a chemical equation as another, what might that mean?

4. When an iron fence rusts, does it lose mass?

5. The opposite of a combustion reaction (like the burning of wood in a campfire) is called synthesis. This is when you take things and mix them together to make a new thing. If I added milk, sugar, eggs and flour together and baked it, I'd get a cake. How would the weight of the cake relate to the weight of the ingredients?

WEEK 4

Physical Science

Newton's 3rd Law

MS-PS2-1

Use observations to explain how birds can use Newton's Third Law to fly.

Directions: Read the text below. Then answer the questions that follow.

What Is Newton's Third Law?

You've likely heard of Sir Issac Newton and his Laws of Motion. Today we are going to focus on his **Third Law** which focuses on the idea of force between two objects. **Force** is any interaction that changes the overall course or movement of an object. For example, if a pitcher throws a baseball at a batter, the force exerted on the ball by the bat changes the direction that ball is moving and the speed at which it travels once it is hit.

Newton's Third Law states that for every action there is an opposite and equal reaction. Another way to think of it is that if object A exerts a force on object B, object B will exert an opposite force on object A. If you jump off a chair into the floor, your legs exert force down on the floor and the floor therefore exerts opposite and equal force back up towards your legs. When a plane engine propels the airplane forward, the airflow is pushing backwardsin order to push the plane forwards.

1. Force will cause what to happen to an object?.

   A. It will always cause the object to get smaller

   B. It will always stop the object

   C. It will always cause the object to speed up

   D. It will always change the movement of the object

2. Newton's third law states that there is an equal and what reaction between two interacting objects?

   A. Forceful

   B. Opposite

   C. Different

   D. Propelling

3. If there was a plate sitting on a countertop, the plate is exerting force down on the countertop. The countertop is doing what?

   A. Exerting no force

   B. Exerting force down on the plate

   C. Exerting force up on the plate

   D. There is not enough information to answer this question

Yesterday, you learned about Newton's Third Law of Motion. Today you will explore forces and how interacting objects exert opposite forces on each other.

Directions: Read each text below and complete the activity. Then answer the question that follows.

The Force On A Balloon

Take a balloon and blow it up but do not tie it off - just pinch the end. Go outside and let the balloon go of the pinched end. Observe the path of the balloon.

1. What force was pushing the balloon around?

Weight & Force

Take a gallon of milk and a small can of soup and place each of them on a scale. Weigh each of them. You can also just use two different sized dumbbells. Now try doing twenty bicep curls with each one and record how many you can do before you get too tired to do more.

2. Which object exerts more force on the scale? Why do you think that?

3. Which object was harder to do more bicep curls with?

Changes In Motion

Take a tennis ball and sit facing a wall about 5 feet away from it. Roll the ball towards the wall with some effort and record what direction the ball bounces back off of the wall. Make sure to roll the ball towards the wall at different angles, sometimes straight on, sometimes from the side. Do this about ten times.

4. Does the ball always bounce back straight at you?

   A. Yes

   B. No

Yesterday, you explored how Newton's Third Law affects different everyday objects. Today you will explain why you observed what you did and how it relates back to Newton's Law.

Directions: Read each text below. Then answer the questions that follow.

The Force On A Balloon

You discovered that releasing air from a balloon will cause it to move around a space until all the air has left the balloon.

1. If the balloon is moving forward, what is the opposite and equal force in this example?

Weight & Force

You discovered that something that weighs more is harder to do more bicep curls with.

2. Which object exerts more force on your arm?

3. When you hold an object and lift your arm up, what is happening in terms of force?

Changes In Motion

You discovered that a ball will bounce back at different angles depending on the angle you from which you rolled the ball into a wall.

4. When you rolled the ball into the wall straight out in front of you, what direction did it bounce back?

Yesterday you explained how Newton's Third Law is demonstrated through the movement of everyday objects. Today you will conduct a series of observations about bird flight and how it relates to the Third Law of Motion.

Materials:

1. A notebook and pencil
2. Binoculars (optional)
3. A computer with internet access

Procedure:

Go outside and observe as many different bird species as you can while they are flying. Use binoculars, if you have them, for more detailed observations, you can also watch videos of birds in flight on the Internet. While observing birds, write down the following observations:

A. How often do they flap their wings? Are they constantly moving their wings or do they flap them only ever so often? Try to quantify your data in seconds.
B. How big are their wings? Try to estimate their wingspan or how big their wings are in comparison to the rest of their body. You can also look this up online.
C. Notice how they move when they are changing direction, taking off, or landing.

Follow-Up Questions:

1. What is the purpose of a bird flapping its wings? Try to relate it back to Newton's Third Law of Motion.

2. What species of bird that you observed had the largest wingspan?

3. What species of bird that you observed had the smallest wingspan?

4. Do all birds flap their wings the same amount? Which bird flapped the most often during flight? Which one flapped the least often?

5. What did you notice about how a bird uses its wings when it changes direction in the air?

Newton's 3rd Law

EXPLAINING THE TOPIC

Yesterday, you observed birds and made some observations about how they fly. Today you will elaborate on these observations and explain how birds use Newton's Third Law of Motion in order to stay airborne during flight.

Directions: Read and answer each question below.

1. When birds fly, what are the opposite but equal forces?

2. When a bird stops flapping its wings but it is still in the air, what do you think is happening?

3. When a bird wants to land, what does it do? Again, try to relate it back to Newton's Third Law of Motion.

4. If a bird has a short wingspan, how does that change how they fly?

5. If you could "design" a bird, how could you make it so that the bird could fly without flapping as often?

WEEK 5

Physical Science

Waves of Light

MS-PS4-2

Make observations to construct an evidence-based account about how waves of light can reflect and move through objects.

Directions: Read the text below. Then answer the questions that follow.

Why does light travel in waves?

When you think of waves, you probably think of a beach and the action of ocean water crashing onto the shore. You may think of the shape of a wave or a surfer riding one in a competition. Light also travels in "waves" but their movement is slightly more complicated.

Light consists of two types of waves: electric and magnetic fields respectively. This is why it is said that light moves in electromagnetic waves. Instead of thinking like light as an ocean wave, however, think of it more like a pattern. Light moves in a constant pattern that cycles up and down.

Different colors of light are different colors precisely because of these cycles or waves. Red light moves very slowly so the cycles or waves are spread out whereas blue light moves very fast so the waves are quicker.

1. Light is made up of the magnetic field and what other field?

   A. Cycle
   B. Pattern
   C. Color
   D. Electric

2. The wave-like way that light moves can also be described as:

   A. A straight line
   B. A cyclical pattern
   C. A circle
   D. Blue or red

3. The color of light is determined by

   A. How long or short the wavelengths are
   B. How powerful it is
   C. How magnetic it is
   D. How much of a pattern it has

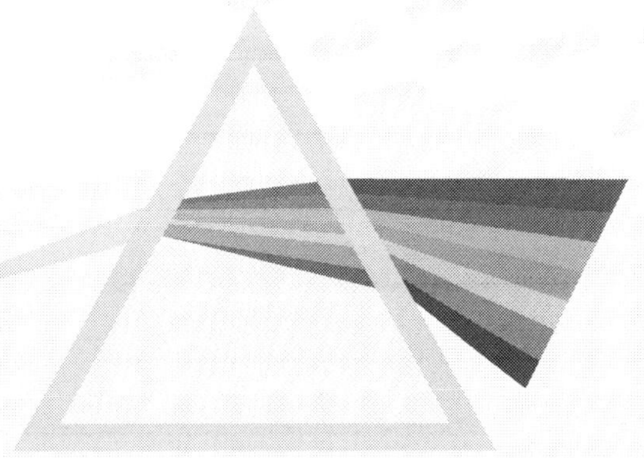

Yesterday, you learned that light moves in a wavelike pattern. Today you will explore how lightwaves travel through different substances.

Directions: Read each text below and complete the activity. Then answer the question that follows.

A Hose Full Of Rainbows

Note: this works best on a very sunny day

Go outside and stand with your back to the sun. Now turn your hoes on as high as it will go. Put your finger over the end of the nozzle so it sprays a fine mist. Hold it up to the light and notice if you see anything new.

1. What colors can you see in the mist of the hose?

Reflection In A Spoon

Find a very shiny spoon in your kitchen, one that is made of a metal. Look at your reflection in the concave side of the spoon, the side that you pick soup up with. Notice the reflection of your face. Now turn it around so you are looking at the convex side of the spoon or the back of the spoon. Again, notice the reflection of your face.

2. Why was it important to use a shiny, metal spoon?

3. What did you notice about your reflection on the front of the spoon compared with your reflection on the back of the spoon?

Double Sunglasses

Take two pairs of cheap sunglasses and hold them about a foot in front of your face so that one pair is directly in front of the other. You should hold one pair in your left hand and one pair in your right hand. You should still be able to see through the two pairs of sunglasses even if it is a bit dark. Now take the pair in your right hand and begin to slowly rotate it 90 degrees, making an X with the two sunglasses.

4. What happens to the light coming through the sunglasses as you rotate them to make an X?

Yesterday, you explored how lightwaves travel through different substances and materials. Today you will explain what happened to the light in these demonstrations.

Directions: Read each text below. Then answer the questions that follow.

A Hose Full Of Rainbows

You discovered that creating a mist of water causes a rainbow of colors to appear.

1. Why do you think a rainbow doesn't show up in a stream of water but it does show up in a mist of water?

Reflection In A Spoon

You discovered that your reflection changes depending on the shape of a reflective object.

2. Why do you think the shape of an object changes the reflection of an image? Relate this to what you understand about how light moves.

Double Sunglasses

You discovered that when you rotate sunglasses 890 degrees when they are parallel to each other, light cannot pass through the polarized lenses.

3. Why do you think light was unable to travel through the two lenses of the sunglasses when they were held at opposite angles to each other?

Yesterday you explained how light travels through and reflects off of surfaces in different ways. Today you will continue to explore how color and temperature are related.

Materials:

1. Two kitchen thermometers
2. 1 piece of white construction paper
3. 1 piece black construction paper
4. A surface outside that is exposed to complete sunlight (a wooden surface is best).

Procedure:

1. Place the two kitchen thermometers on top of the outside surface on a sunny day.
2. Let the thermometers sit there for about 15 minutes and then record the temperature of both of them. They should read the same temperature - if not it may mean that one of them is damaged or that they are sitting on two different types of materials.
3. Place a piece of black construction paper on top of one thermometer, making sure to completely cover the entire thermometer. Then immediatly place a piece of white construction paper on top of the other thermometer, making sure to completely cover the entire thermometer.
4. Wait 30 minutes. Record the temperature of each thermometer at the end of 30 minutes and then place the same piece of paper back over the thermometer.
5. Wait another 30 minutes and then record the temperature of each thermometer again.

Follow-Up Questions:

1. Why was it important to let the thermometers sit outside for 15 minutes before covering them?

....

....

....

2. Which thermometer had a higher temperature after 30 minutes?

....

....

....

3. Which thermometer had a higher temperature after 60 minutes?

4. Which paper was warmer to the touch when you lifted it off the thermometer at the end?

5. Go online and research the colors black and white. How does light interact with white objects and with black objects? The word "reflect" should be somewhere in your answer.

6. Why does light make some objects warmer?

Waves of Light

ELABORATING ON THE TOPIC

Yesterday, you observed how light can impact the temperature of different colored objects. Today you will elaborate on these conclusions.

Directions: Read and answer each question below.

1. What is the relationship between light and thermal energy?

2. Why did the black paper make the thermometer's temperature rise?

3. Why is it bad to walk your dog on asphalt on a hot, sunny summer day?

4. If you wanted to design a car that didn't overheat in the summer, what color would you make it?

5. What is a similarity between the shiny spoon you experimented with on day #2 and the white piece of paper from day #4?

WEEK 6

Life Science

Physiology & The Nervous System

MS-LS1-8

Make observations to construct an evidence-based account about how the nervous system functions.

Directions: Read the text below. Then answer the questions that follow.

How Does The Nervous System Work?

Our body has many ways in which it takes in information from the outside world and makes sense of it. The physiological system that is most involved in this process is the nervous system. The nervous system is composed of your brain and connects to the rest of your body through your **neurons.** Your brain and spinal cord make up your **Central Nervous System (CNS)** and your neurons (found everywhere else in the body) make up your **Peripheral Nervous System (PNS).**

The process of how your nervous system functions can be broken down into three steps:

1. Neurons in the Peripheral Nervous System take in information from your surroundings through the five senses of touch, taste, smell, sight and hearing.
2. That information is delivered to the Central Nervous System where it is processed and it is determined how you will respond to this information, if at all.
3. Your brain sends that decision back to the Peripheral Nervous System and your body responds appropriately.

1. What structures are found in the PNS?

   A. Brain
   B. Spinal Cord
   C. Sight
   D. Neurons

2. Your CNS contains your brain as well as your

   A. Neurons
   B. Sense of smell
   C. Spinal cord
   D. Sense of taste

3. Which word best describes what the brain does with information in step #2?

   A. Processes
   B. Senses
   C. Changes
   D. Disregards

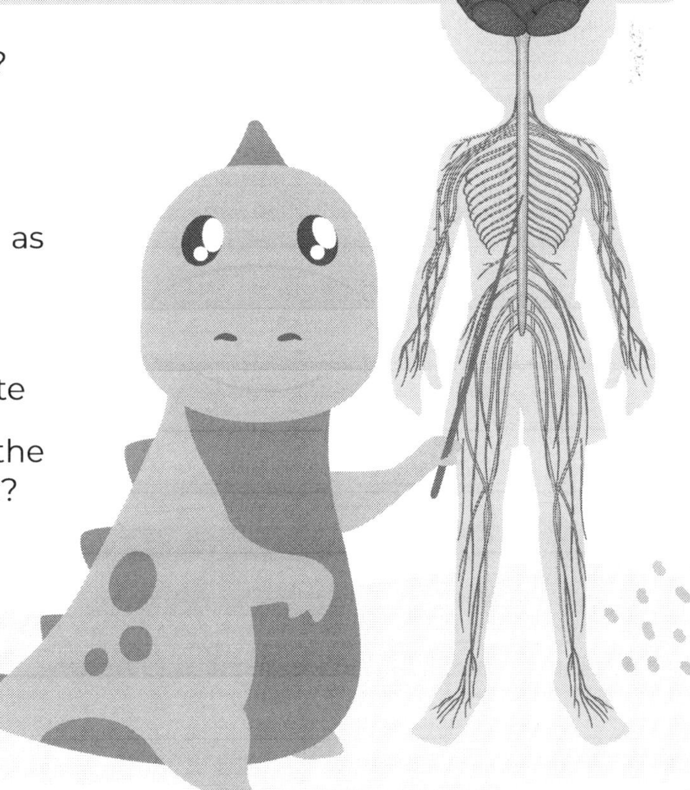

Yesterday, you learned about the Nervous System and how it processes information. Today you will explore how your nervous system interprets information.

Directions: Read each text below and complete the activity. Then answer the question that follows.

Reflexes & Sight

This demonstration works best with a friend or parent. Stand across from your partner with your arm stretched out in front of you at shoulder height. Have them hold a ruler just above your open hand perpendicular to the floor. The lowest number should be closest to yoru top finger. Without telling you, they will let go and you will try to catch the falling ruler as quickly as you can. Record what inch mark your thumb falls (1 inch = roughly 1 millisecond). Complete 10 times.

1. On average, how many milliseconds did it take you to catch the ruler?

Warm Hand Vs. Cold Hand

Take about a hundred pennies and spread them out in one layer on a table. Set a timer and then pick up as many as you can in 30 seconds. Count the pennies and record your total. Do this 3 more times. Next, submerge your hands in a cold bowl of water for 60-90 seconds. Quickly wipe them dry and then pick up pennies again for 30 seconds. Record your total. Repeat 3 more times, chilling your hands between each trial.

2. How did your penny totals compare between having warm hands and cold hands?

Poke A Partner

This demonstration works best with a friend or parent. You'll need two sharpened pencils. Have your partner alternate gently poking you with 1 or 2 pencils at the same time on the back of your neck without telling you how many pencils they are using. Record if you are correct or not correct and complete 6 times. Now, have them complete that process again on the back of your arm and the palm of your hand, making sure your eyes are closed during the trials - you want to rely on your sense of touch, not your sense of sight.

3. On what part of your body - your neck, arm, or palm - were you able to differentiate between 1 and 2 pencil pokes most accurately?

Physiology & The Nervous System

EXPLAINING THE TOPIC

Yesterday, you explored the how your body processes and responds to touch and sight as well as the idea of reflexes. Today you will explain the conclusions you can draw from those demonstrations.

Directions: Read each text below. Then answer the questions that follow.

Reflexes & Sight

You discovered that it took at least a few milliseconds to catch the ruler after you saw it begin to fall.

1. Why does it take time to catch the falling ruler?

Warm Hand Vs. Cold Hand

You discovered that it is harder to pick up pennies with cold hands than with warmer hands.

2. How might the temperature of your hands affect your nervous system?

Poke A Partner

You discovered that you were able to accurately differentiate between 1 and 2 simultaneous pencil pokes most accurately with the back of your palm.

3. Why do you think your sense of touch on your palm is more accurate than the back of your neck or the back of your arm?

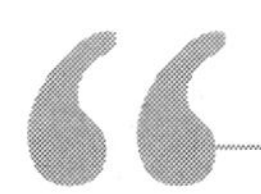

Yesterday you explained how the nervous system works based on observations from demos you conducted the previous day. Today you will experiment further on your own nervous system and determine more about how it functions.

Materials:

1. A partner (parent, friend, sibling, etc).
2. 8 -10 different food items which have a strong smell (pick things that aren't very messy - potato chip, peeled banana, ground coffee, chocolate chip cookie, vinegar, etc.)
3. 8-10 identical bowls or cups (plastic is fine).

Procedure:

1. Place a small amount of each food in their own cup.There should be one cup of each food - do not mix foods.
2. Exit the room and have your partner arrange the cups of food in a line.
3. Come back into the room and only by looking at the cups, take 90 seconds to memorize the order of the items of food.
4. Close your eyes and say the order out loud. Your partner will write down how many you get correct.
5. Now exit the room again and your partner will rearrange the food into a different order.
6. With your eyes closed, have your partner lead you into the room and have you smell each food item in order. You again have 90 seconds to memorize the order. Again they will ask you to repeat the order with your eyes closed and write down how many you get correct.
7. Exit the room a final time and your partner will rearrange the food. When you come back in you should both look at and smell the order of the food. After 90 seconds, close your eyes and repeat the order. Your partner will write down how many you got correct.

Follow-Up Questions:

1. How many food items did you get correct when you could only look at them?

....

....

....

2. How many food items did you get correct when you could only smell them?

3. How many food items did you get correct when you could both look at and smell them?

4. Were there foods that were always easy to remember? What were they?

5. Were there foods that were always difficult to remember? What were they?

6. Would this experiment be harder or easier if you used only one type of food - for example they were all different types of fruits?

Yesterday, you experimented with memory and your sense of touch and smell. Today you will try to elaborate on your findings and draw some final conclusions about how your nervous system processes information and even stores it as a memory.

Directions: Read and answer each question below.

1. What was the pathway of information through the Nervous System when you saw a food item that you needed to memorize? Make sure to mention the PNS and CNS in your answer.

2. What was the pathway of information through the Nervous System when you smelled a food item that you needed to memorize? Make sure to mention the PNS and CNS in your answer.

3. When you remembered the order of the food items, what was happening in your nervous system?

4. Why might it be easier to remembember food that you both saw and smelled at the same time.

5. How can experiences become memories?

6. Would you trust a witness who was next to a victim when a crime was committed or a witness who heard the crime happen from a block away? Relate your answer to our senses and to memory.

WEEK 7

Life Science

Ecosystems & Populations

MS-LS2-4

Read texts and use media to explore how keystone species' populations affect ecosystems.

Directions: Read the text below. Then answer the questions that follow.

How Does The Environment Affect Populations?

The environment contains living **(biotic)** and non-living **(abiotic)** things. Some abiotic components of the environment could be animals, plants, fungi and even bacteria. Some abiotic components include water, rocks,sunlight, and soil. Both biotic and abiotic aspects of the environment directly impact the organisms living in these environments. Today we are looking at ecosystems and how changes in an ecosystem can cause a change in the populations of organisms.

An ecosystem is a defined area and all of the biotic and abiotic factors included in that area. For example, your ecosystem includes your house, your family, the vegetables that you eat, and everything else that you come into contact with or use as a resource. A **population** on the other hand is the number of individuals of one species living in a defined area. If we look at humans, we could define a population in a number of ways. We could look at the population of a whole country, a single state, a city or even just a household. **Populations are made up of only one kind of living thing in a specific place.**

1. Which one of these would be considered a biotic factor:

   A. Mushroom
   B. Wind
   C. Sand
   D. Dead leaf

2. An ecosystem must contain biotic factors and what else?

   A. Only a single population
   B. Rocks
   C. A country
   D. Abiotic factors

3. Populations are made up of .... and defined to a particular area.

   A. Abiotic factors
   B. A single species of organism
   C. Ecosystems
   D. Resources

Yesterday, you learned about ecosystems and what they contain as well as the definition of a population. Today you will explore how the environment affects populations.

Directions: Read each text below and complete the activity. Then answer the question that follows.

Space & Populations

Take a cup or a container that size and fill it with dried beans. These beans represent a population of deer. Count how many you could fit in the cup and write it down. Now add 5 large marshmallows - these represent a new housing development in the ecosystem of the deer. Add as many of the beans as you can to fill the cup again and then count the beans that could fit. Write this number down.

1. How many less beans could fit in the cup after the marshmallows were added.

Food & Populations

Take those same beans and place ten in front of you to represent ten deer. Let's say that one deer eats 2 marshmellows of food per a year which is equal to 400lbs of food. Place two marshmallows in front of each bean. Now take three pennies and place them in front of you - these represent foxes and they eat 200lb of food a year. They eat the same type of food as deer. Do not add anymore marshmallows to the table the marshmallows on the table are the only food in this ecosystem.

2. How many foxes can one marshmallow feed per a year?

   A. 1
   B. 2
   C. 3

3. Is there enough food in this ecosystem to feed all of the animals?

   A. Yes
   B. No

Predators & Populations

Let's say you have a population of rabbits. Let's say this year a population of wolves, their natural predator in this ecosystem, increased significantly.

4. What will happen to the population of the rabbits which, in this example, are considered prey?

   A. Increase

   B. Decrease

   C. Stay the same

Yesterday, you explored how populations change in response to their ecosystem. Today you will explain why these changes occurred.

Directions: Read each text below. Then answer the questions that follow.

Space & Populations

You discovered that when space is limited in an ecosystem, a population of organisms will decrease.

1. Why do you think housing developments negatively impact populations?

Food & Populations

You discovered that when food is limited, it can negatively impact a population, especially if more than one population uses that same resource.

2. Explain how a population might deal with a decrease in the amount of food available in their ecosystem?

Predators & Populations

You discovered that an increase in a population of predators can cause a decrease in the population of prey animals.

3. If the wolves ate all of the rabbits, what would happen to the wolf population?

You have spent several days learning about, exploring and explaining how changes in an ecosystem can affect populations. Today you will look at data about a single population and draw some conclusions from in.

Background Information:

In Southern Montana there is a population valley which is home to a native species of prairie coneflower. Generally these prairie coneflowers do very well in this climate. Below you will read over data about the population of the prairie coneflowers in this valley, the weather, and the population of aphids in this valley. Aphids are small insects which feed off of and eventually kill these species of flowers.

Data:

Year	Population of Prairie Coneflowers	Average Annual Temperature (F)	Population of Aphids
2012	3,820	75	1,384,938
2013	3,825	76	1,309,384
2014	2,700	67	1,299,973
2015	2,799	72	1,367,592
2016	3,230	74	1,287,950
2017	2,236	74	1,897,294
2018	2,221	74	2,390,819
2019	3,490	76	1,792,493

Follow-Up Questions:

1. During what year was the Prairie Coneflower population highest?

2. During what year did the average annual temperature seem most irregular?

3. What was the largest population for the Aphids and during which year did it occur?

4. In what year did you see the first decline in the Prairie Coneflower population?

5. In 2019, what was happening to the population of the Prairie Coneflower?

6. Between 2016 and, 2017 what happened to the Aphid population?

Yesterday, you analyzed data about the Prairie Coneflower and aspects of its ecosystem. Today you will elaborate on your findings and draw some general conclusions about how changes to an ecosystem can affect a population of organisms.

Directions: Read and answer each question below.

1. Why do you think the population of Prairie Coneflowers decreased in 2017? What does this tell you about abiotic factors in this ecosystem?

2. Can the population of one organism affect the population of another organism? Justify your answer.

3. Why do you think there was a decline in the population of Aphids after 2018?

4. If farmers in this valley began to spray pesticides, killing off Aphids, what would you expect to see happen?

5. If the average annual temperature rose to 79° in 2020 and 2021, what do you predict would happen to the Prairie Coneflower population?

WEEK 8

Life Science

Biodiversity

MS-LS4-5

Read texts and use media to determine the need to protect biodiversity both for ethical and other reasons.

Directions: Read the text below. Then answer the questions that follow.

What is Biodiversity?

Since life began on this planet over 4.5 billion years ago, countless different species of plants, animals, fungi, bacteria and protists have evolved to fit every type of ecosystem Earth has to offer. Even within the species of human you can see there is a vast amount of variety in terms of just what people look like. The most beautiful thing about life on our planet is that it comes in so many different forms.

Biodiversity is the variety of life found in a given area. If there is high biodiversity, it means there are lots of different species of living things. If there is low biodiversity, there are not many different species in an area. Biodiversity is one of the most important things that we need to protect on this planet. Throughout this week, you will learn about biodiversity and how maintaining it positively impacts the economy, medicine, science and society as a whole.

1. How long ago did life begin on planet Earth?
   - **A.** Two million years ago
   - **B.** Four and a half million years ago
   - **C.** Forty five million years ago
   - **D.** Four and a half billion years ago

2. Biodiversity is a measure of how much .... of living species there are in an area.
   - **A.** Evolution
   - **B.** Variety
   - **C.** Population
   - **D.** Biology

3. True or false: protecting biodiversity can have a positive impact on the economy?
   - **A.** True
   - **B.** False

Yesterday, you learned about biodiversity and the benefits of maintaining it. Today you will explore biodiversity in your local environment as well as a bit about global biodiversity.

Directions: Read each text below and complete the activity. Then answer the question that follows.

Biodiversity In A The Park

Go to a local green space or park - an area that is relatively undeveloped by humans. Take 30 minutes to count as many different organisms as you can - include animals, plants, mushrooms, insects and anything else that is alive. You don't have to identify them by their exact name, just count them if they are different from anything else you see.

1. How many different living organisms did you count?

Biodiversity In Developed Area

Go to the center of your town or city - try to find an area that has a lot of buildings or has been developed by humans such as the business district or a shopping center. Take 30 minutes to count as many different organisms as you can - include animals, plants, mushrooms, insects and anything else that is alive. You don't have to identify them by their exact name, just count them if they are different from anything else you see.

2. How many different living organisms did you count?

Amounts Of Biodiversity In Different Ecosystems

Use the internet to look up these three different ecosystems: desert, rainforest, and the tundra. Research how much biodiversity each of these ecosystems have. Another way to approach this question is to look up how many different kinds of species they are home to. Record your findings.

3. Which ecosystem has the most biodiversity?

4. Which ecosystem has the least biodiversity?

Yesterday, you explored the level of biodiversity in different areas of the world. Today you will try to explain why biodiversity can change depending on where in the world you look.

Directions: Read each text below. Then answer the questions that follow.

Biodiversity In The Park

You discovered that parks and green spaces tend to have more biodiversity.

1. Why do you think there is more biodiversity in this area?

Biodiversity In Developed Area

You discovered that areas developed by humans tend to have lower amounts of biodiversity.

2. Why do you think there is less biodiversity in this area?

Amounts Of Biodiversity In Different Ecosystems

You discovered that the rainforest tends to have the most number of species (high biodiversity) and that the desert and the tundra has the lowest number of species (low biodiversity).

3. What about the rainforest makes it a great ecosystem for lots of biodiversity to develop and thrive?

4. What about the tundra and desert makes it hard for biodiversity to exist?

Week 8 Biodiversity

Day 4 EXPERIMENTING WITH THE TOPIC

Yesterday you explained why different parts of the world have more or less biodiversity. Today you will analyze data on how biodiversity can impact different aspects of society including the economy and conservation.

Background Information:

Below you will find different areas of the world, the type of ecosystem they have, their main form of economic income and how much money they put towards biodiversity should this be defined efforts. Please read through the data and answer the questions below:

Place	Ecosystem(s)	Total number of species	Economic Income By Sector	Conservation budget
South Africa	Grasslands, Savannah	Over 100,000	Mining	Over $600 million
New Zealand	Temperate Broadleaf Forests	Over 70,000	Manufacturing and agriculture	Over $500 million
Canada	Boreal Forest, Tundra, Grassland and Deciduous Forests	Over 80,000	Oil and gas; tourism	Over $10 billion annually

Follow-Up Questions:

1. What country or countries have grassland ecosystems?

....

....

....

2. Which country has the most biodiversity?

....

....

....

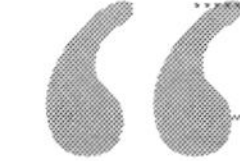

3. What are the main forms of economic income for Canada?

4. How much does New Zealand's government spend on conservation annually?

5. What country spends the most on conservation?

6. South African makes a good portion of its income from what sector?

Yesterday, you analyzed biodiversity in three different countries as well as their economies. Today you will elaborate on some of that data and draw final conclusions about how protecting biodiversity impacts different aspects of society.

Directions: Read and answer each question below.

1. Why might Canada need or choose to spend over $100 billion on conservation every year?

2. Do you believe South Africa should spend more, less or the same amount on conservation as they currently are spending annually? Feel free to research a bit more about conservation in South Africa before answering this opinion-based question.

3. Which of these sectors is impacted by changes in biodiversity?

4. What might be an unintended consequence if biodiversity is not protected?

5. Why might the number of species in New Zealand be smaller than in Canada?

WEEK 9

Life Science

Modeling Evolution

MS-LS4-6

Make observations and gather information about how different populations of organisms evolve to best fit their environment.

Directions: Read the text below. Then answer the questions that follow.

Can Populations Change Over Time?

Since life began 4.5 million years ago, tons of biodiversity has evolved all over the planet as was discussed in Week #8. In order to understand how changes occur, we must understand the principle of natural selection. Natural selection is the driving force behind the theory of evolution. When an organism evolves it is so that it can have traits that are beneficial and help it survive in the environment. Those traits allow that organism to gain more resources, survive predators, any other other number of benefits. As a result they are able to reproduce more and pass that trait on to the next generation, altering the population a little bit. So, in conclusion, nature selections for the best traits in a population of organisms.

Let's look at an example of natural selection. Let's say there is a population of beetles that, at some point in history, came in the colors green and red. The green beetles were able to camouflage better amongst the plants while the red beetles were easy to spot and got eaten by birds. Since the green beetles survived better, they passed their green color trait on to the next generation of beetles. Today this population of beetles is only green and the red color is no longer found in this population. Nature selected for the green color and against the red color in beetles.

1. What ultimately causes changes in a population?

   A. Evolution
   B. Biodiversity
   C. Natural Selection
   D. Traits

2. Which of the following are traits that natural selection would favor?

   A. Bigger claws for protection
   B. Camouflage in habitat
   C. Heightened sense of smell for finding food
   D. All of the above

3. True or false: natural selection selected against the green beetle color trait?

   A. True
   B. False

Yesterday, you learned how the process of evolution is driven by natural selection and how this can cause changes in populations of living organisms over time. Today you will explore examples of this in plants, animals and bacteria.

Directions: Read each text below and complete the activity. Then answer the question that follows.

Evolution Of Orchids

Orchids are one of the most diverse groups of flowers in the world. *Ophrys apifera*, known in Europe as the Bee Orchid, has evolved to look like bees. Over time, the shape and color of its petals changes little by little to resemble the shape and color of bees. Other orchids have evolved to be attractive to beetles, hummingbirds, and even bats.

1. What traits is natural selection selecting for in the orchid?

2. Why do you think it is beneficial for orchids to be attractive to insects, birds and bats?

Vestigial Organs In Humans

During our early evolution, before we knew how to use fire to cook our food, humans ate raw meat and vegetation. In order to tear this very tough food, we developed our wisdom teeth. Today, however, we no longer eat much raw meat. As a result, our wisdom teeth are considered **vestigial structures.** Vestigial structures are parts of an organism that have lost their function because that organism no longer uses the environment in the same way.

3. Once an organism evolves a trait, will it always need it?

Antibiotic Resistance In Bacteria

Tuberculosis is a terrible respiratory disease caused by the bacteria *Mycobacterium tuberculosis*. There are many different strains of this bacteria, each one that can only be treated by certain types of antibiotics. Recently a few strains of the tuberculosis bacteria have been found to be completely resistant to any antibiotic that humans have created.

4. Do all populations or strains of *Mycobacterium tuberculosis* have the same traits?

Yesterday, you explored the different ways that natural selection can alter populations of plants, bacteria and even humans. Today you will explain why some of those changes occured.

Directions: Read each text below. Then answer the questions that follow.

Evolution Of Orchids

You discovered that orchids have evolved to look like their pollinators

1. If an orchid looks like a pollinator, how does that benefit the orchid?

Vestigial Organs In Humans

You discovered that vestigial structures are no longer used by an organism.

2. 2. Do you think over time humans could lose their wisdom teeth all together?

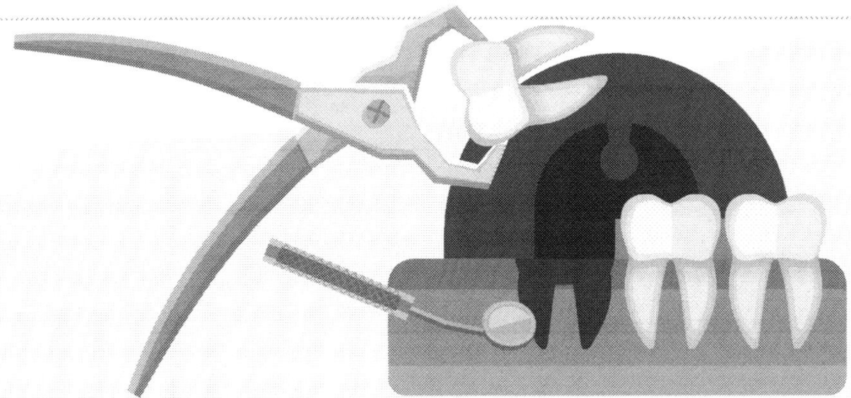

Antibiotic Resistance In Bacteria

You discovered that the bacteria that causes tuberculosis comes in different strains and that some trains cannot be eradicated by using antibiotics.

3. How do you think *Mycobacterium tuberculosis* has evolved so many strains/ populations of different types of bacteria?

4. Why is antibiotic resistance a problem for human health?

Modeling Evolution

EXPERIMENTING WITH THE TOPIC

Yesterday you explained how natural selection causes changes in different populations of organisms. Today you will analyze data from a population of organisms to see mathematically how change can occur over time.

Background Information:

Below you will find data for a population of salamanders. In this population, there are three sizes of salamanders - small, medium and large ones. Salamanders usually live and hide amongst small pebbles near riverbeds. The natural predator of salamanders in this habitat is the blue heron.

Year	# of Small Salamanders	# of Medium Salamanders	# of Large Salamanders	# of Blue Heron	Square Feet of Riverbed
1990	240	180	530	56	1400
2000	279	199	329	63	1387
2010	388	184	98	59	1212

Follow-Up Questions:

1. How many years passed between each recording of data?

2. What happened to the number of small salamanders in the population over time?

3. What happened to the number of medium salamanders in the population over time?

4. What happened to the number of large salamanders in the population over time?

5. What happened to the number of blue herons in this habitat over time?

6. What happened to the area of the riverbed over time over time?

Week 9 Modeling Evolution

Day 5 ELABORATING ON THE TOPIC

Yesterday, you analyzed a population of salamanders and the changes that occured in that population over time. Today you will elaborate on those findings and draw conclusions about now natural selection can increase or decrease certain traits in a population over time.

Directions: Read and answer each question below.

1. Why do you think the small salamanders survived best?

2. What happened to the physical environment that caused changes in the salamander population?

3. What happened to the blue heron population and how might it have affected the salamander population?

4. What do you think will happen to the salamander population in the next 50 to 100 years?

5. Do you think evolution is a fast process? Why or why not?

WEEK 10

Life Science

Genetic Modification

MS-LS2-5

Read texts and use media to explore how bioengineering is changing the agriculture, namely GMOs.

Directions: Read the text below. Then answer the questions that follow.

What Are GMOs?

Each and every organism in this world has its own unique **genome.** A genome is the collection of DNA that an organism has in each of its cells and it codes for all the characteristics of its genome. Each genome can contain thousands if not hundreds of thousands of different genes. Genes are traits and, in humans, can determine things like eye color, ear lobe shape, toe length and everything else in between.

Genetically Modified Organisms, also known as GMOs, are living things that have had their genomes modified. Scientists have figured out how to isolate many genes in different species and then control them so that they cause different or new traits to occur. For example, scientists have altered the DNA of a species of tomatoes so that they do not spoil quickly. Scientists can also take genes from one organism and add them into the genome of another organism. The gene for human insulin production was put into bacteria so that bacteria can be used to produce insulin for patients with diabetes.

1. The collection of an organism's entire set of DNA is called
   - **A.** A gene
   - **B.** A genome
   - **C.** A trait
   - **D.** A GMO
2. A gene determines an organism's
   - **A.** Entire genome
   - **B.** DNA
   - **C.** Traits
   - **D.** Insulin production
3. True or false: you can take genes from one organism and put them into a different organism's genome?
   - **A.** True
   - **B.** False

Week 10 Genetic Modification

Day 2 EXPLORING THE TOPIC

Yesterday, you learned about genomes and how traits are controlled by genes in living organisms. You also learned what a GMO is. Today you will explore GMOs further.

Directions: Read each text below and complete the activity. Then answer the question that follows.

GMOs In The Home

Go into your pantry and grab ten different products. Now look at the packaging and see if you can find a label that says "Non - GMO certified" or something that indicates whether or not it contains GMO products in it.

1. How many products did you find in your pantry that state they are "Non GMO certified"?

GMOs & Medicine

As mentioned yesterday, GMOs have been used to help make medicine for patients. Go online and research the hepatitis B vaccine produced with GM baker's yeast.

2. What is hepatitis B?

   A. A virus
   B. A bacteria
   C. A fungus
   D. A yeast

3. Are people who are allergic to yeast allergic to the hepatitis B vaccine?

   A. Yes
   B. No
   C. They can be, it depends on the person

GMOs & Public Health

Animals can also be genetically modified. Mosquitoes are being genetically modified in order to stop their ability to spread certain diseases, specifically malaria. Go online and research GMO mosquitos.

4. True or false - malaria is caused by a Plasmodium parasite that the mosquito carries, not the mosquito themselves.

   A. True
   B. False

Week 10 Genetic Modification

Day 3 EXPLAINING THE TOPIC

Yesterday, you explored how GMOs can be used in different aspects of our lives including food, medicine, and disease control. Today you will explain some of your findings. Note: feel free to go back to the websites you used for research yesterday and use those to help with your explanation.

Directions: Read each text below. Then answer the questions that follow.

GMOs In The Home

You discovered that some of your pantry items might not contain GMOs.

1. Why do you think food items might contain GMOs?

2. Why do you think people might want GMO products to be labeled?

GMOs & Medicine

You discovered that some medicines are produced with the help of GMOs.

3. What are some drawbacks to GMO-produced medicines?

GMOs & Public Health

You discovered that GMO mosquitoes can help stop the spread of malaria.

4. Do you think it is ethical to genetically modify an animal to help protect humans?

Week 10 Genetic Modification

Day 4 EXPERIMENTING WITH THE TOPIC

Yesterday you explained some of the benefits and drawbacks to GMO organisms. Today you will experiment with some of these ideas and look at the pros and cons of a specific GMO.

Background Information: Golden Rice

Golden rice is a species of GMO plant that was created in the late 1990s. Scientists Peter Beyer and Ingo Potrykus developed this GMO to be able to make its own carotenoids, a molecule that when ingested by humans, produces Vitamin A. The goal was to help stop malnutrition in regions where rice can easily be grown such as Vietnam and the Philippines. Since its development, various pros and cons related to Golden Rice have been found:

Pros	**Cons**
Combats malnutrition with carotenoids	Monocropping (countries that farm Golden Rice might stop planing other species of rice and lose biodiversity as a result)
Helps the economy by preventing blindness and improving agriculture	Carotenoids are not the most important nutrient in our diets
No known negative environmental impact	We are unsure how golden rice's genome impacts our own genome

Follow-Up Questions:

1. What is your understanding of monocropping and why is a loss of biodiversity bad?

....

....

....

....

2. Why does preventing blindness help the economy?

....

....

....

3. What do carotenoids become when humans eat them?

4. How might golden rice impact our genome?

5. Why is it important that golden rice not impact the environment?

Week 10 Genetic Modification

Day 5 ELABORATING ON THE TOPIC

Yesterday, you analyzed the story of Golden Rice and considered the pros and cons of its use. Today you will elaborate on these ideas and draw further conclusions about GMOs.

Directions: Read and answer each question below.

1. Are GMOs good or bad?

2. What are some positive things that GMOs can do for the world?

3. What are some negative things that GMOs can do for the world?

4. If you wanted to create a GMO, what do you have to know about an organism first?

5. Let's say you were asked to create a GMO that could be sold to people who were looking to make their own clothing. What kind of a GMO would you design and why? Consider the pros and cons of your GMO concept.

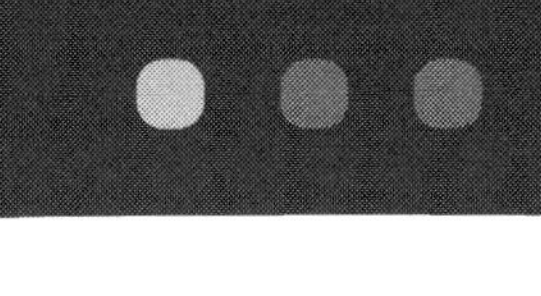

WEEK 11

Earth & Space Science

Scaling The Solar System

MS-ESS1-3

Use tools and materials to design and build a scale model of your solar system.

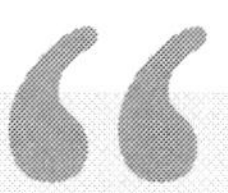

Scaling The Solar System

ENGAGING WITH THE TOPIC

Directions: Read the text below. Then answer the questions that follow.

How Big Is Our Solar System?

Our solar system is a small part of the Milky Way Galaxy, just one of an estimated 2 billion to 2 trillion galaxies in the whole universe. Our solar system is a massive place and contains 1 star, 8 planets, more than 150 moons and countless asteroids, comets and even dwarf planets. In order to contain that much stuff, you need a lot of space!

In 1977, NASA launched Voyager One, a space probe which is still to this day traveling across space at around 35,000 miles per hour! About 35 years later it was able to pull away from the gravitational cloud of the sun, but it was still in our solar system. Scientists estimate that it will take Voyager One another 40,000 years to officially make it to the outermost part of our solar system!

Our solar system is so large that miles and meters simply can't be used to express how big space is. Astronomers use **Astronomical Units (AU)** in order to express distances. One Astronomical Unit is equal to the average distance between Earth and the Sun and is equal to about 150 million kilometers.

1. About how many moons are there in our solar system?

A. 1
B. 8
C. 150
D. 2 billion

2. What is the name of the space probe launched by NASA in 1977?

A. Voyager One
B. Milky Way
C. Astronomical Unit
D. Solaris

3. How long is one Astronomical Unit?

A. 1,500 kilometers
B. 1,500,000 kilometers
C. 150,000,000 kilometers
D. 150 kilometers

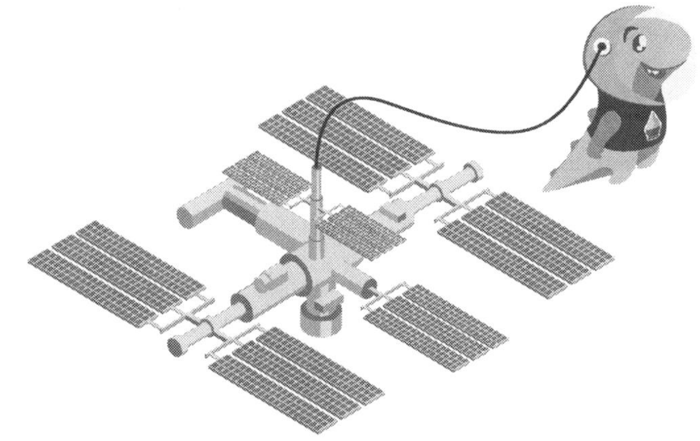

Scaling The Solar System

EXPLORING THE TOPIC

Yesterday, you learned that our solar system is really large and contains a lot of different objects including planets, moons and other things. Today you will explore the vastness of space and the concept of scaling. Scaling is when you take something and make it proportionally larger or proportionally smaller.

Directions: Read each text below and complete the activity. Then answer the question that follows.

Scaling Down

Take a meter stick and measure your height in centimeters, or have someone measure your height for you. Record your height. Let's say you want to draw a picture of yourself on a piece of copy paper. In order for it to fit, you need to scale your height down. Let's say that every 10cm of your actual height now equals 1cm on your drawn picture of yourself. The conversion factor is 10cm for every 1cm.

1. How many inches tall would your drawn image be if you scaled your actual height down? Remember 10cm of your height = 1cm in your drawing.

Scaling Up

Now let's say you want to put a picture of yourself on a huge billboard on the side of the highway. The billboard is 9 meters tall or 900cm. Let's now saw that we want to scale your image up so that it fills most of the billboard. In order to do that, 10cm of your actual height now equals 100cm of your billboard image. The conversion factor is 10cm for every 100cm.

2. How many inches tall would your billboard image be if you scaled your actual height up? Remember 10cm of your height = 100cm in your billboard.

Scaling Distances

Grab a meter stick and measure the width of your room or the distance between the two furthest points in your room. Now think back to the scale we used in the first activity where 10cm in distance equals 1cm in a drawing on a piece of copy paper. Draw a picture of your room as if you were looking down on it from a bird's eye view.

3. If you were to draw a picture of your room to scale, how many centimeters in width would you need to measure on your drawing? Remember 10cm the conversion factor of your height = 1cm in your drawing.

Scaling The Solar System

EXPLAINING THE TOPIC

Yesterday, you explored how to scale measurements up and how to scale them down. Today you will explain how scaling could be used to explore the distances between objects, including parts of our solar system.

Directions: Read each text below. Then answer the questions that follow.

Scaling Down

You discovered that in order to scale down an item, you need to find a conversion factor that reduces the size of an objection proportionally.

1. How did you determine the conversion factor?

2. How could this be used to scale a planet from our solar system in a drawing?

Scaling Up

You discovered that in order to scale up an item, you need to find a conversion factor that increases the size of an objection proportionally.

3. If you wanted to triple a recipe for chocolate chip cookies, could you scale it up even though it is not measured in centimeters?

Scaling Distances

You discovered that in order to scale down a distance between two items, you need to find a conversion factor that reduces the distance between two points proportionally.

4. How could this be used to scale the distance between the Earth and the Sun in a drawing?

Yesterday you explained how you can use scaling to increase or decrease the size of an object or a distance. Today you will try scaling distances in our solar system, specifically distances from the sun to the planets.

Materials:

1. A piece of string of yarn that is about 5 meters in length
2. Beads of different sizes and colors (you should be able to thread the string/yarn through them)
3. A centimeter ruler and/or a meter stick
4. A calculator

Procedure:

1. Complete the chart below by converting the distances from the sun into centimeters. Remember, distances are in AU (astronomical units) which equal 150 million kilometers so we will need to scale things down considerable. In this activity, let's have a conversion factor where 1 AU = 10 cm.
2. Once you've filled in the chart, pick a bead to represent each planet.
3. Place the sun at the end of the sting and then measure all of your distances from there. String your bead onto the string and knot it to the measured distance to keep it in place.
4. When you are done, observe the string and the relative distances between all of the planets.

Planet/Star	Distance in AU	Distance in cm (scaled down)
Sun	0.0 AU	0.0 cm
Mercury	0.4 AU	
Venus	0.7 AU	
Earth	1.0 AU	
Mars	1.5 AU	
Jupiter	5.2 AU	
Saturn	9.6 AU	
Uranus	19.2 AU	
Neptune	30 AU	
Pluto	39.5 AU	

Week 11 Scaling The Solar System

Day 4 EXPERIMENTING WITH THE TOPIC

Follow-Up Questions:

1. Why does the sun measure 0.0 AU or 0.0 cm?

2. What planet is 2nd closest to the sun?

3. What two planets are closest to each other?

4. How many centimeters are Mars and Saturn from each other?

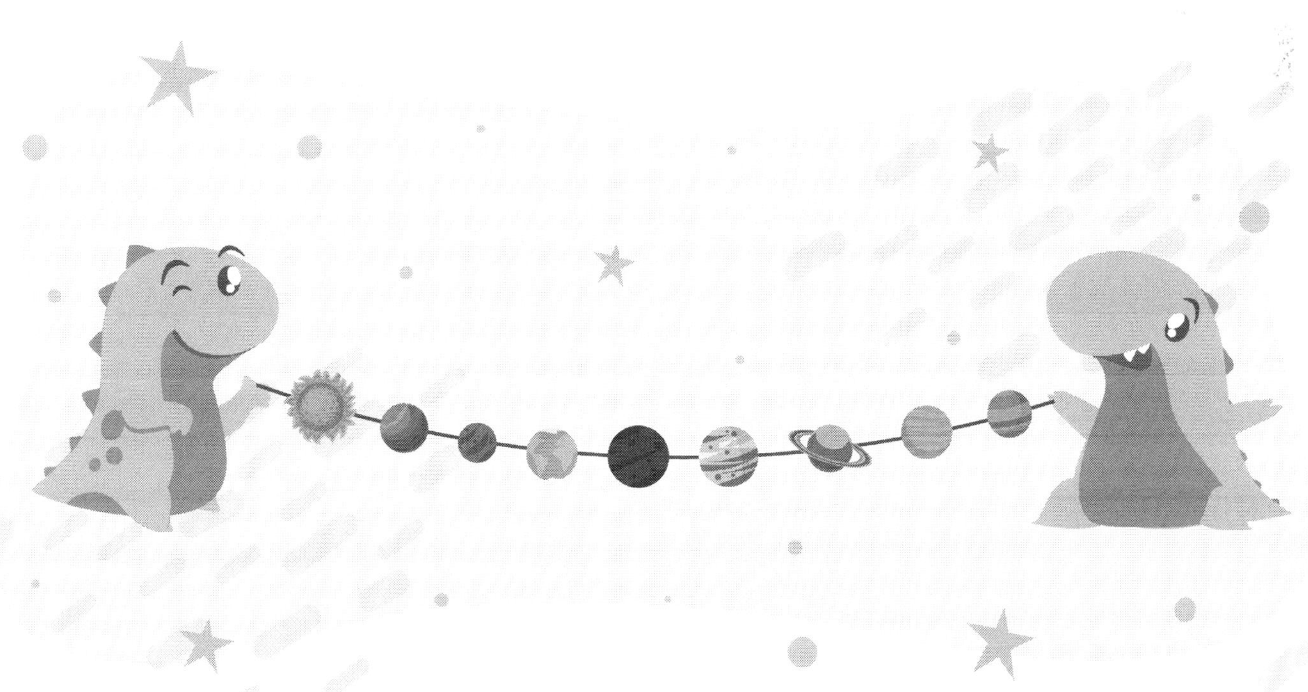

Week 11 — Day 5

Scaling The Solar System

ELABORATING ON THE TOPIC

Yesterday, you created a scaled down model of the solar system and its planets. Today you willelabroate on observations from this activity and draw some conclusions about the scale of our solar system.

Directions: Read and answer each question below.

1. Is the distance between each planet the same between all planets?

2. What is the solar system mostly composed of and why?

3. If you wanted your scale model to be more accurate, what could you do?

4. If you were going to use a football field as the outer limits of the solar system, what would you have to determine the conversion factor?

5. An image taken by a telescope of an asteroid that is far away is going to be smaller than the asteroid itself. How can scaling be used to estimate the size of the asteroid?

6. If you had a model of a spaceship, could you scale it up to be the actual size of a real spaceship?

WEEK 12

Earth & Space Science

Changes In Earth's Surface Over Time

MS-ESS2-2

Use observations of local geography and research other biomes to explore how geoscientific processes have changed Earth's surface over time.

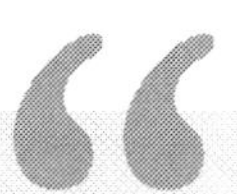

Directions: Read the text below. Then answer the questions that follow.

Hutton & Lyell

Earth has not always looked like it does today. Large events such as earthquakes, volcanic eruptions and meteors have caused huge changes on Earth's surface. There are also smaller events that occur regularly such as landslides and geothermal reactions that slowly alter the surface of the planet. It may be obvious to you that Earth's surface has gone through a ton of change over time, but up until just over 150 years ago, most people did not believe that.

Thanks to the work of **James Hutton** and **Charles Lyell,** two scientists working in the 1800s, the theory of uniformitarianism was created. They believed that Earth was constantly changing, mostly through small events. One piece of evidence found by Lyell that supported this was fossils of seashells on the top of a mountain range. He believed that mountains had once been below sea level and that as the mountain range developed over millions of years,the fossils moved with it. This groundbreaking theory of **uniformitarianism** also influenced the famous evolutionary scientist Charles Darwin - if Earth could change slowly over millions of years, so too could living organisms from generation to generation. This epiphany helped him refine his theory of evolution.

1. Which of these is an example of a small event that changes Earth's surface?

   A. Meteor
   B. Volcano
   C. Earthquake
   D. Geothermal reaction

2. What theory suggests that Earth is constantly changing, mostly through small events?

   A. Evolution
   B. Uniformitarianism
   C. Landslide
   D. Creationism

3. What other theory was developed thanks to the work of Hutton and Lyell?

   A. Evolution
   B. Uniformitarianism
   C. Landslide
   D. Creationism

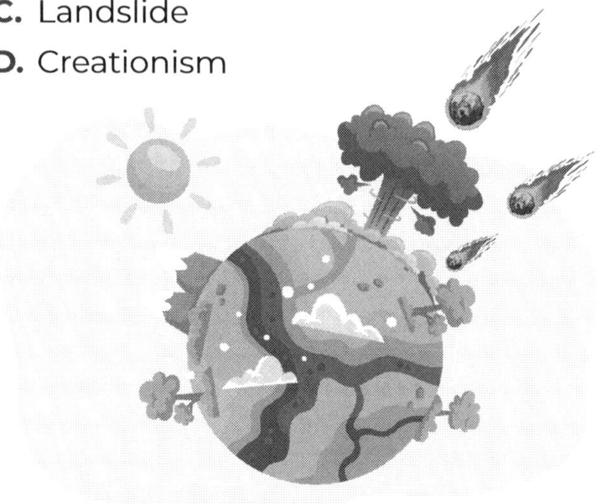

Yesterday, you learned about the work of Hutton and Lyell and how it led to the theory of uniformitarianism. Today you will explore how Earth's surface can change through both large and small events through a few activities and demonstrations.

Directions: Read each text below and complete the activity. Then answer the question that follows.

Layers of Lava

Warning! hot glue

Take a piece of cardboard and a hot glue gun and make a small mound of glue in the center of it to represent a volcano. Let it dry and then sketch the outline of it on a piece of paper looking at it from one side. Now drizzle about a quarter-sized amount of hot glue over it. Wait 30 seconds for it to dry and then sketch the outline of the resulting volcano. Repeat this process of drizzling glue and drawing the outline of the resulting volcano 5 times.

1. What do you think the glue represents?

2. What did the volcano look like by the end of the activity?

Unearthed Treasure

Make sure to do this outside as it can get messy. Take a shoebox and place 5 small objects in the bottom of it - a quarter, a golf ball, or anything like that. Now fill the box almost to the top with dry sand. Now shake the box for 20 seconds. Record if any of your objects appear at the top of the sand. If not, shake the box for another 20 seconds and record if anything surfaced at the top. Do this for about 10 rounds or until you are able to uncover at least one of the objects.

3. How long did it take for you to unearth one of your objects by shaking the box?

Weather & Erosion

Using the sand from the previous activity, build a small sandcastle or simple sand mound on a level surface outside. It should be at least 6 inches tall. Fill a spray bottle with water. Hold the spray bottle about six inches above the top of the sandmound and spray it 10 times. Record any changes you see. Repeat the process of spraying and recording visual changes to your sand castle for about 15 rounds.

4. What changes did you see happen to the sand mound over the 15 rounds?

Yesterday, you explored how Earth's surface can change due to events and processes. Today you will explain why those changes occurred and how time was a factor in these changes.

Directions: : Read each text below. Then answer the questions that follow.

Layers of Lava

You discovered that the shape of a volcano changes with each eruption of lava.

1. Over time, how could volcanic eruptions change the surface of Earth?

Unearthed Treasure

You discovered that shaking a box of sand will unearth objects that were once buried in the sand.

2. What did the shaking of the box represent?

3. How could earthquakes be used to learn about things below Earth's surface?

Weather & Erosion

You discovered that water can change the shape of a solid structure such as a sandcastle. This is known as **erosion**.

4. What did the spray bottle of water represent?

5. If a mountain was located in an area of the world that started to experience a lot of rainfall over many hundreds of thousands of years, what might happen to the mountain?

Yesterday you explained how different processes can change the surface of the Earth either relatively quickly, or slowly over thousands or millions of years. Today you will experiment with how canyons can form over time.

Materials:

1. A clear plastic box (such as Tupperware) that is about the size of a shoebox or a little bigger
2. Between 7-10 different colors of sand
   A. You want enough sand in total to fill the box about halfway to the top. This sand can be purchased at craft and hobby stores. You can also make different colors of sand by adding a few drops of food coloring to regular sand and mixing it up in a closed ziplock bag.
3. A water bottle with a narrow spout
4. A spray bottle with water.

Procedure:

1. Place each color of sand in the box one layer at a time. Be careful not to mix the layers/ colors of sand together. When you look at the box from the side you should see each individual layer of colored sand easily - these layers are called strata in geology!
2. At one of the shorter sides of the box, start pouring a small, thin stream of water. Watch the sand as you do this and refill the water bottle as many times as you need to to make a small canyon in the sand. Remember, always pout the water from the exact same spot on one end of the box.
3. Once you have a canyon, look at the strata in the canyon. Also observe the sand at the opposite end of the box from where you poured the water.
4. Lastly, spray the canyon from the top with water from the water bottle - spray it about 40 times. Observe any changes that occurred in and around your canyon.

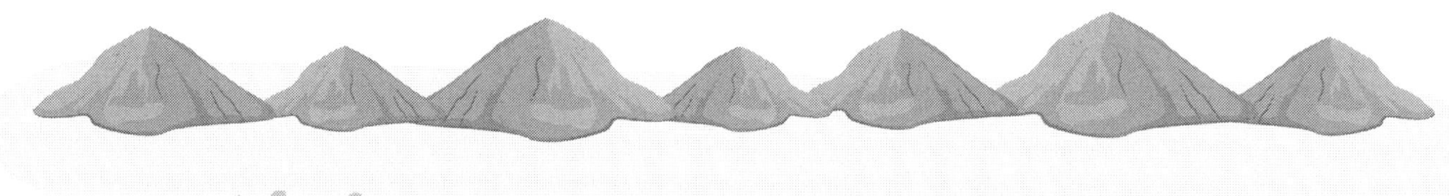

Follow-Up Questions:

1. What does the colored sand represent?

2. Why is it important not to mix the sand?

3. What does the water from the water bottle represent?

4. What does the water from the spray bottle represent?

5. What do you notice about how the canyon looks on the inside of it?

Changes In Earth's Surface Over Time

ELABORATING ON THE TOPIC

Yesterday, you created a model of a canyon. Today you will elaborate on this demonstration and draw conclusions about the processes that change Earth's surface over time.

Directions: Read and answer each question below.

1. Do you think canyons form from quick, large events or slow, steady processes? Why?

2. What could slow down the formation of a canyon?

3. Where does the Earth carved out of a canyon go?

4. How could global warming impact changes on Earth's surface?

5. What could cause a canyon to change a lot very quickly?

WEEK 13

Earth & Space Science

Cycling Of Water On Earth

MS-ESS2-4

Use tools and materials to design a model of how water cycles on Earth.

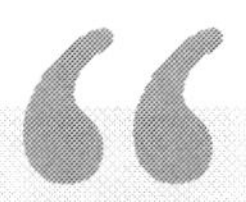

Directions: Read the text below. Then answer the questions that follow.

The Water Cycle

Water is arguably one of, if not the most important compound on Earth. Organisms require water to live, landscapes are shaped by the flow of water, and Earth's temperature is impacted by water in all of its forms. Understanding how water cycles allows us to understand more about nearly every aspect of the natural world.

The Water Cycle can be broken down simply into a few major stages. Since this is a cycle, water can enter it at any point. Water evaporates from Earth's surface, meaning it turns from a liquid to a gas or, more accurately, water vapor. As water rises into the atmosphere, it cools down and condenses. Depending on the temperature and other conditions, it will turn back into a liquid (rain) or become a solid (show and ice). Water then falls back to Earth's surface as precipitation and can collect in streams, rivers, ponds, lakes, and oceans. Water can also be used by plants and animals for various processes but will eventually end up back in the water cycle.

1. Which of these is water an important part of?
   - **A.** Earth's temperature
   - **B.** Living organisms
   - **C.** The shaping of landscapes
   - **D.** All of the above

2. When water turns into a gas this is known as
   - **A.** Condensation
   - **B.** Precipitation
   - **C.** Ice
   - **D.** Vapor

3. When water falls back to Earth's surface after condensing in the atmosphere this is called
   - **A.** Precipitation
   - **B.** Condensation
   - **C.** Evaporation
   - **D.** Uniformitarianism

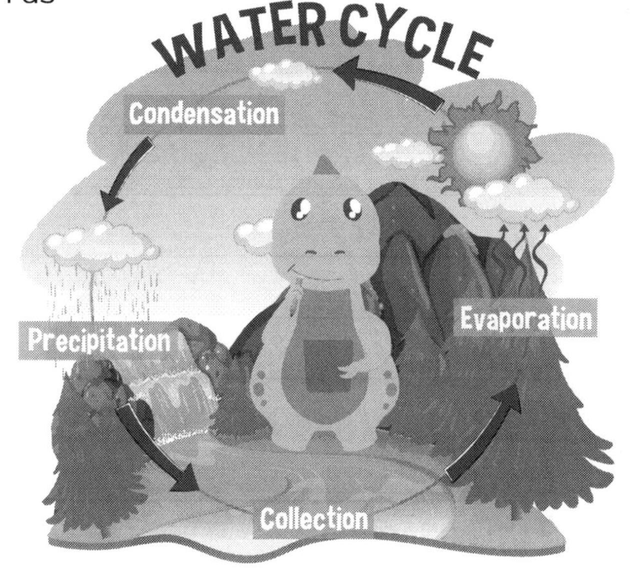

Yesterday, you learned about the water cycle and its importance on Earth. Today you will explore the major steps that happen in the water cycle through hands-on demonstrations.

Directions: Read each text below and complete the activity. Then answer the question that follows.

What's Up Water

Take a clear bowl and pour an inch of hot water into it. Immediately cover it with plastic wrap and place 2 ice cubes on top of the plastic above the center of the bowl. Watch the bowl for about 5-10 minutes and notice any changes that occur.

1. What happens to the underside of the plastic wrap?

Cloud In A Bottle

*Note: have a parent present when using matches

Take an empty plastic soda bottle (2 litres is best) and fill it with about 2 inches of very warm water. Put the cap on the bottle. Shake the bottle for 10 seconds and then put it down and watch it for two minutes. Now pick it up and shake it again for 10 seconds. Immediately light a match, let it burn for a few seconds, and blow the match out. Drop it into the bottle and put the cap back on. Observe the bottle for another two minutes.

2. What happens when you add a match to the bottle after it has been shaken?

Where Did The Water Go?

Take two clear plastic cups and fill them with an inch of room temperature water each. Place one cup in direct sunlight and place the other cup in a dark cupboard or a place with no sunlight. Leave them and come back in 24 hours to check on them. Measure the height of the water in each cup.

3. Which cup lost more water?

Yesterday, you explored how water condenses, precipitates and evaporates. Today you will explain why these phenomena happened.

Directions: Read each text below. Then answer the questions that follow.

What's Up Water

You discovered that hot water will condense on the underside of plastic that is chilled with ice.

1. What process of the water cycle does this represent?

2. Why is it important to use the ice?

Cloud In A Bottle

You discovered that a lit match placed in a bottle with water vapor will cause a cloud to form.

3. What did the shaking of the bottle do?

4. Why did the match cause a cloud to form? What did it provide?

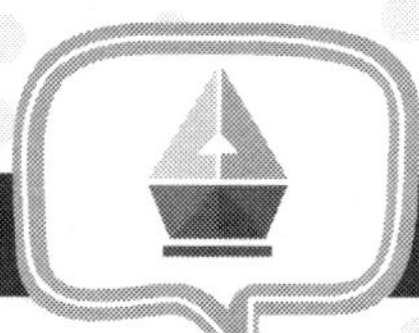

Where Did The Water Go?

You discovered that water placed in direct sunlight evaporates faster than water placed in no sunlight.

5. Why do you think water in direct sunlight evaporates faster?

Week 13 Cycling Of Materials On Earth

Day 4 EXPERIMENTING WITH THE TOPIC

Yesterday you explained why different aspects of the water cycles occur. Today you will look at data from different parts of the world to see how the water cycle changes based on the environment.

Background Information:

Below is a table of water-related data from three different states in the U.S. from the past 10 years. Analyze the data table and then answer the follow-up questions below.

Data Table:

Location (U.S. State)	Average Annual Temperature	Average Annual Rainfall	Average Annual Snowfall	Average Annual Erosion Rate (tons per acre)	Percent Land Covered By Agriculture
Hawaii	70.0 °F	63.7 inches	0 inches	100+	40%
New Mexico	53.4 °F	14.6 inches	22.74 inches	9.7	58%
Oregon	48.4 °F	27.4 inches	10.91 inches	5.2	28%

Follow-Up Questions:

1. What state has the most rainfall annually?

2. What state experiences the most erosion?

3. Which state has the lowest average annual temperature?

4. Which state has the most land covered by agriculture?

5. What is the average annual snowfall in Oregon?

6. What percent of Hawaii's land is dedicated to agriculture?

ELABORATING ON THE TOPIC

Yesterday, you analyzed water cycle data about three different states. Today you will elaborate on your conclusions and relate them to how the water cycle functions.

Directions: Read and answer each question below.

1. Why do you think Hawaii experiences the most rainfall?

2. Why do you think Oregon experiences more rain than snowfall annually?

3. Why do you think Hawaii has the most erosion of the three states?

4. What about New Mexico's climate makes it good for agriculture? What aspects of the climate are not as beneficial?

5. If climate change caused Oregon's annual temperature to rise 10°F higher annually, what changes might happen to the water cycle in this state?

WEEK 14

Earth & Space Science

Climate Change

MS-ESS3-5

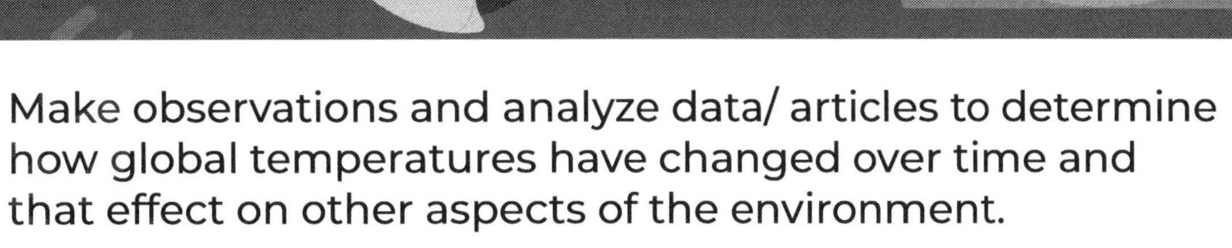

Make observations and analyze data/ articles to determine how global temperatures have changed over time and that effect on other aspects of the environment.

Week 14 Climate Change

Day 1 ENGAGING WITH THE TOPIC

Directions: Read the text below. Then answer the questions that follow.

What Is Causing Climate Change?

Over the past few lessons you have learned that the environment, living organisms, and climate are all linked together. You have likely heard about **climate change** before. In order to understand climate change, you need to first understand climate. Oftentimes weather and climate are used interchangeably but they are in fact phenomemon. Weather is the day-to-day changes that are short term - think a single thunderstorm, a heat wave, or a blizzard. Climate is the long-term pattern in weather for specific regions of the world. The climate in Southern California is warm and dry for most of the year whereas the climate in Alaska is cold and snowy for the majority of the year.

Climate change is when these regional patterns of weather change noticeably. Changes in climate are most often caused by human activities such as pollution, greenhouse gases, and other factors that greatly impact the atmosphere. Climate change can negatively impact so many different entities within the environment, both living and nonliving, as you will see throughout this lesson.

1. Climate is best described as

   A. Short term changes
   B. Extreme storms
   C. Long term patterns
   D. Global

2. Which of the following would be considered weather

   A. Annual rainfall for a particular state
   B. The average temperature over a decade in a country
   C. A hailstorm
   D. All of the above

3. Which of the following can negatively impact the environment?

   A. Greenhouse gases
   B. Pollution
   C. Long-term changes in climate
   D. All of the above

Yesterday, you learned about the difference between weather and climate.You also learned that climate change can impact the environment negatively. Today you will explore climate change with some hands on demonstrations and activities.

Directions: Read each text below and complete the activity. Then answer the question that follows.

Measuring Your Water Intake

Take a moment and consider how much water you use in a day. You drink water, you brush your teeth, you use the toilet, and you wash your hands just to name a few things. Laundry and cooking require a fair amount of water as well. Spend the day trying to estimate how much water you use and use the internet to research average amounts of water usage for different activities.

1. How much water do you estimate that you use in a single day?

Modeling Greenhouse Gases

Take two clear plastic cups and fill them with an inch of room temperature water each. Place both of them in direct sunlight but place one in a clear ziplock bag. The ziplock bag represents the layer of greenhouse gases that let light from the sun in and trap heat as well. Leave the cups for two hours then come back and measure the temperature of the water.

2. Which cup contains warmer water?

Losing Our Ice Caps

Fill two identical clear plastic bowls with 2 cups of room temperature water and place both bowls in direct sunlight. Measure the temperature of each bowl and record their starting temperatures - they should have the same temperature. Now place a piece of dark blue construction paper so that it covers one bowl and a piece of whtie construction paper on the other bowl. The white paper represents our polar ice caps and the blue paper represents the open ocean. Leave the bowls for a couple hours then come back and measure their temperatures.

3. Which bowl has warmer water in it at the end of the demonstration?

Yesterday, you explored various issues related to climate change. Today you will explain their significance when it comes to climate change.

Directions: Read each text below. Then answer the questions that follow.

Measuring Your Water Intake

You discovered that you use a lot of water every single day.

1. How do you think human water usage could impact climate change? Consider doing some research on the internet to help inform your answer.

2. What are three different ways you could actively reduce your daily water usage?

Modeling Greenhouse Gases

You discovered that greenhouse gases (modeled by a ziplock bag) trap heat and cause water temperatures to rise.

3. What could be a negative impact of global water temperatures rising?

Losing Our Ice Caps

You discovered that water placed under a dark blue paper (representing open ocean) will heat up faster than water covered by white paper (representing polar ice caps).

4. Why do you think the melting and disappearing of glaciers and polar ice caps is impacting global climate change?

Yesterday you explained how different aspects of climate change can be bad for the planet. Today you will analyze some climate change data.

Background Information:

Below is a table of water-related data from three different states in the U.S. from the past 10 years. Analyze the data table and then answer the follow-up questions below. ***Note:** extreme precipitation events include blizzards, hurricanes, and other incidents where abnormal rainfall was experienced.

Year	Average Global Temperature Change	Average Number Of Extreme Precipitation Events in US	Greenhouse Gas Emissions (in billions of tons)	Number of Extinct Species	Human Population (in billions)
1900	0.0 °F	8	2	2,000	1.6
1950	0.4 °F	8	5	5,000	2.58
1990	0.5 °F	22	20	20,000	5.33
2019	1.0 °F	42	35	50,000	7.71

Follow-Up Questions:

1. In what year did the planet experience the biggest increase in global annual temperature? How many degrees?

2. How many extreme precipitation events occured in the United States in 1950? What about in 1990?

3. How many more billions of tons of greenhouse gases were produced in 2019 than in 1990?

4. About how many species are extinct today?

5. Between 1950 and 1990 what happened to the human population?

ELABORATING ON THE TOPIC

Yesterday, you analyzed data about global changes to climate and other environmental factors. Today you will elaborate on these findings and explain how the impact of climate change is supported by scientific data.

Directions: Read and answer each question below. Make sure to use the data to support your claims.

1. Why do you think the average global temperature is increasing more and more each year?

2. How are other organisms besides humans being affected by changes to the global climate and/or environment?

3. Do you think the human population can/should grow at this rate forever?

4. In terms of major extreme weather events, what is happening? Why do you think this is happening?

5. If we were able to reduce our greenhouse gas emissions to 10 billion tons by 2030, what impacts do you think that could have for global climate change?

WEEK 15

Earth & Space Science

Human Impact On Resources

MS-ESS3-4

Read texts and use media to compare how populations of three different countries differ and how it impacts resource usage.

Directions: Read the text below. Then answer the questions that follow.

How Human Needs Impact The Environment

Think about everything that you use on a daily basis - food, water, space for your home, electricity and clothing are just a few needs. Every day humans use resources. All of our resources come from the environment which means that human use of resources has a huge impact on the natural world.

There are two types of resources out there. **Renewable resource**s are resources that we can make or extract more of from the environment indefinitely. These include things like solar power, wind power, geothermal heat, and agriculture. The speed at which we can make or get more of these resources vary so it is important to consider the amount of human use versus the amount of resources that the environment can support.

The other type of resource is **nonrenewable resources.** These are resources that once we delete them, the planet will not provide any more. This includes nuclear power, fossil fuels, coal, natural gas and most raw minerals and elements. In this lesson you will learn why it is important for humans to minimize their resource usage and how overuse can negatively impact other living creatures.

1. Which of these is an example of a resource you use on a daily basis?

   A. Food
   B. Water
   C. Shelter
   D. All of the above

2. ______________ resources can be made or extracted from the environment indefinitely.

   A. Fossil fuel
   B. Renewable
   C. Nonrenewable
   D. Minerals

3. True or False: Our use of both renewable and nonrenewable resources can impact other living creatures?

   A. True
   B. False

Yesterday, you learned about the difference between renewable and nonrenewable resources. Today you will spend time looking at how many resources you use every day.

Directions: Read each text below and complete the activity. Then answer the question that follows.

Measuring Your Energy Intake

Take a moment and consider how much energy you use in a day. Electricity, gas and heat are all forms of energy. Write down a list of everything you use or come into contact every day that uses at least one of these forms of energy.

1. What are some things you use energy for every day?

Measuring Your Waste

Every day we use things and then don't need them any more. Take a plastic gallon ziplock bag and carry it around with you for the day. Any time you go to throw something away, place it in the ziplock bag instead. At the end of the day, weigh the bag on a kitchen scale.

2. What was the most common type of trash you throw away on a daily basis?

3. How much did your bag weigh at the end of the day?

So Much Space...or is it?

Take a piece of graph paper and place it in front of you. Now take 10 dried black beans and 10 dried pinto beans and place them on the graph paper. Each black bean represents a wild animal and needs 1 square to survive. Each pinto bean represents 1 human and a human needs 20 squares of graph paper in order to survive. Now place 20 more pinto beans on the paper, arranging all of the beans so that they can all fit and have as many squares as they need.

4. Were all of the beans able to fit by the end of the activity?

Yesterday, you explored various issues related to human resource usage including energy, waste and space. Today you will explain why human resource usage can be problematic for Earth.

Directions: Read each text below. Then answer the questions that follow.

Measuring Your Energy Intake

You discovered that you use a lot of energy every day in different ways.

1. What is the most common form of energy you use? Heat, electricity or gas?

2. What could you do to minimize the amount of energy you use every day?

Measuring Your Waste

You discovered that you generate a fair amount of garbage every day.

3. What can people do to minimize the amount of garbage they make in a day?

So Much Space...or is it?

You discovered that the space use of one species of organisms can impact the amount of space available to other organisms.

4. Why do humans require so many more squares on the graph paper?

5. If you continued to add beans to the paper, what would eventually happen and what does that represent?

Human Impact On Resources

EXPERIMENTING WITH THE TOPIC

Yesterday you explained how different aspects of human resource usage can be bad for the environment. Today you will analyze some data to determine how humans impact both renewable and nonrenewable resources.

Background Information:

Below is a table comparing the United States and New Zealand. The table includes different forms of energy consumption, energy productions (oil) and household demographics.

Data Table:

	United States	New Zealand
Energy Consumption Per Capita	300 BTU per person	250 BTU
% Renewable Energy	17%	40%
% Nonrenewable energy	83%	60%
Barrels of crude oil produced in a day	About 11 million	About 43,906
Average home size	2,600 square feet	2,206 square feet
Average family size	3.14 people	2.7 people

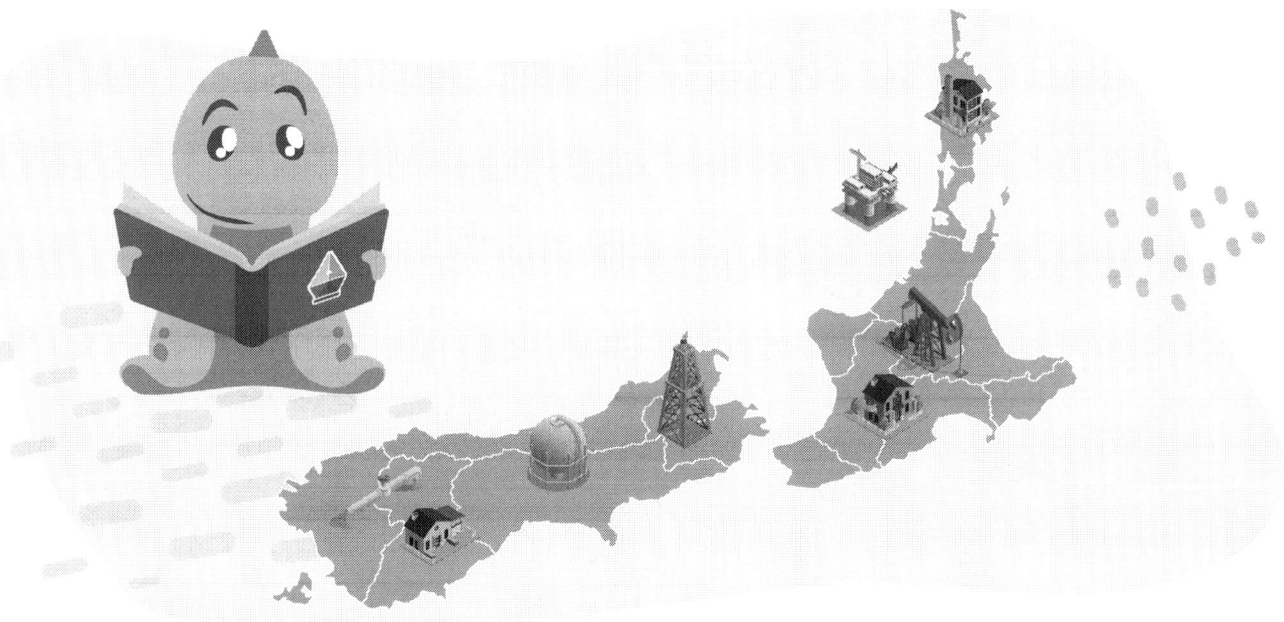

Follow-Up Questions:

1. Which country has the lowest average energy consumption per capita?

2. Which country produces the most crude oil per day?

3. What percent of the United States' energy is renewable?

4. Which country has the smallest home size on average?

5. Why are average family sizes not reported as whole numbers?

6. How much more nonrenewable energy does the United States use compared with New Zealand?

Human Impact On Resources

ELABORATING ON THE TOPIC

Yesterday, you analyzed data about resource usage in the United States and New Zealand. Today you will elaborate on your findings and draw conclusions about how human resource usage can impact the environemnt.

Directions: Read and answer each question below. Make sure to use the data to support your claims.

1. What is one reason you can see in the data that New Zealand might have a lower energy consumption per capita?

2. Is crude oil a renewable or nonrenewable resource?

3. Why does having a larger home lead to more resource usage?

4. What are some of the forms of renewable energy that New Zealand uses? Feel free to research online to answer this.

5. If the United States started producing more solar powered electric cars, what might change about this data table?

6. If New Zealand's populations saw a 30% increase, what might change in regards New Zealand's resource usage?

WEEK 16

Engineering

Identifying The Problem

MS-ETS1-1

Make observations about a product or problem which could be improved through the use of scientific principles.

Week 16

Day 1

Identifying The Problem

ENGAGING WITH THE TOPIC

Directions: Read the text below. Then answer the questions that follow.

How To Identify A Problem...With Science!

Take a moment to consider something you use every day. A toothbrush perhaps? You might have a toothbrush that has hard bristles or one that has soft bristles. You may have a manual toothbrush or one that is powered with batteries. Some toothbrushes have different shaped handles in order to fit your hand better - this is called **ergonomics.** There are so many different kinds of toothbrushes because companies have tried to develop models that fit different people's needs.

When creating or redesigning a product, or even a solution to a problem, the first thing you need to do is identify a potential problem or issue. In the case of a toothbrush, perhaps one problem that came up with that the bristles were too hard and hurt to use - so someone created a toothbrush with softer bristles. Another problem that was identified was that manual brushes weren't removing enough plaque from teeth so someone tried to solve that problem but creating battery-operated toothbrushes.

In this lesson you will learn how to identify problems so that you can begin to engineer solutions to them using your scientific skills and abilities.

1. Which of these best describes something that would be modified using "ergonomics"?

   A. Battery-operated
   B. Soft bristles
   C. Shape of a handle
   D. A toothbrush color

2. Before redesigning a product, what must you do?

   A. Make observations
   B. Ask questions
   C. Collect data
   D. All of the above

3. In the example of the toothbrush, what solution was created to help improve plaque removal?

   A. Battery-operated
   B. Soft bristles
   C. Shape of a handle
   D. A toothbrush color

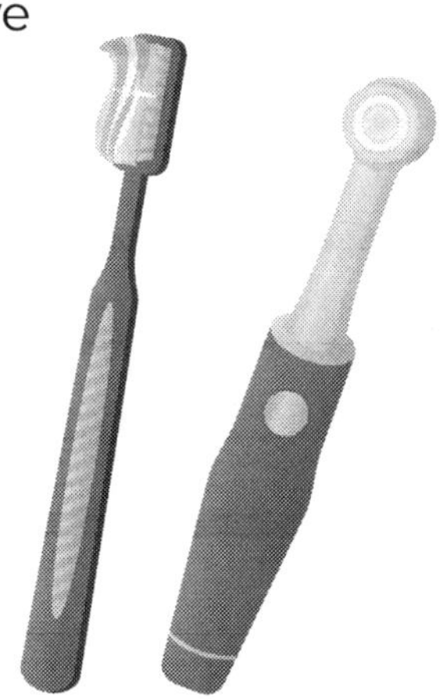

Yesterday, you learned the importance of identifying a problem before proposing a solution. Today you will read through three examples of products or issues and identify the problem.

Directions: Read each text below and analyze for a solution. Then answer the question that follows.

Declining Population

A housing company builds a new development in what was once an open field of wildflowers. This was home to pollinators, such as bees and birds, as well as small rodents like field mice and voles. Nearby farmers are seeing a decline in their harvests and they think it might have to do with this new housing development?

1. What problem are the farmers experiencing?

2. What change in the environment might have led to the farmers' problem?

A Better Bag

Karen has recently started using reusable shopping bags in order to be more eco-friendly at the grocery store. Karen notices that if she puts too many groceries in her reusable cottons bag, the bag will rip open. She can only put about 3 lbs of groceries in it before the bag rips.

3. What is the problem Karen is having with the design of the bag?

Designing For Everyone

Ollie loves to look up at the stars so he buys a telescope so he can see the stars and planets more clearly at night. Ollie sets up the telescope on his balcony and begins to adjust it so he can see clearly. All of the adjustment knobs are on the right-hand side of the telescope. Because Ollie is left-handed, he has to step around the telescope to make adjustments and then step back in front of it to see if they worked. It takes Ollie at least 20 minutes to get the telescope focused on one object, twice as long as it would take someone... twice as long as someone who can make the adjustments with their right hand.

4. What is the problem with the design of the telescope?

Yesterday, you explored various issues and products and identified problems with them. Today you will explain what changes might be made in order to solve the problem.

Directions: Read each text below. Then answer the questions that follow.

Declining Population

You identified that farmers experience poorer crop yields when the habitat of local pollinators is impacted by a housing development.

1. What might be a solution that can help both the pollinators and the farmers?

A Better Bag

You identified that Karen's eco-friendly bag was not strong enough to hold the weight of groceries.

2. What are two changes that could be made to the design of the bag to help improve the bag's strength?

Designing For Everyone

You identified that Ollie was having trouble adjusting his new telescope because it was designed for someone who is right-handed.

3. How could the telescope be redesigned in order to solve this problem?

4. Why is it important to design projects for people with different abilities?

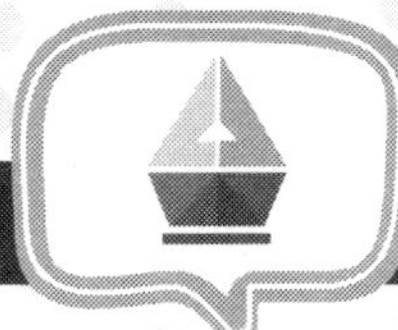

Identifying The Problem

EXPERIMENTING WITH THE TOPIC

Yesterday you explained how different problems could be solved and why it is important to make things accessible for everyone. Today you will experiment on identifying problems with a common household item.

Materials:

1. A No. 2 pencil (one that needs to be sharpened with a sharpener)
2. A mechanical pencil
3. A few pieces of lined paper
4. An eraser

Procedure:

1. Take each pencil and write your full name 10 times on a piece of paper with each pencil using your dominant hand. Your dominant hand is the one you normally write with. Don't pause, just keep writing.
2. Now hold the pencil in your nondominant hand and repeat that process.
3. Erase one copy of your name that you wrote with the No. 2 pencil and one copy of your name that you wrote with the mechanical pencil.

Follow-Up Questions:

1. Which pencil did you write your name with first?

....

2. Which pencil, if either, felt more comfortable in your hand?

....

3. Which pencil were you able to write with longer before the point got dull?

....

4. Which pencil did you write your name with that was harder to erase?

....

5. Which pencil was easier to write with using your non-dominant hand?

....

6. Do you think pencils are designed for people with different dominant hands? Why or why not?

....

....

Week 16 Identifying The Problem

Day 5 ELABORATING ON THE TOPIC

Yesterday, you compared different aspects of mechanical and nonmechanical pencils. Today you will elaborate on your findings and provide suggestions for redesigning this object.

Directions: Read and answer each question below.

1. Why does identifying a problem first make the most sense when addressing an issue or a product?

2. Why do you think mechanical pencils were invented?

3. Why do you think lead refills for mechanical pencils were invented? What problem(s) does this solve?

Identifying The Problem

ELABORATING ON THE TOPIC

4. What is one thing that you think could be improved on the mechanical pencil?

5. What is one thing that could change about pencils to make them better for left-handed people?

6. If you wanted to make mechanical pencils more eco-friendly, what could you do?

WEEK 17

Engineering

Creating a Solution

MS-ETS1-2

Develop a model or an illustration that proposes a solution to the product or problem, clearly defining how its form relates to its function.

Directions: Read the text below. Then answer the questions that follow.

Creating The Best Solution To An Issue

Last lesson you explored how to identify a problem. Once a problem is identified, you can begin to develop solutions to that problem. In science, this correlates strongly with The Scientific Method. The Scientific Method is an organized, step-by-step process that allows us to explore natural phenomena so that we can learn more about our world. It also allows us to develop new products and solutions to issues that may need to be solved.

Once a problem is identified, the first thing that occurs in the Scientific Method is creating a **hypothesis.** This is an educated theory as to why something occurs. Then, a **procedure** or an experiment is developed so that you can test your hypothesis. From this experiment you get **data** and then the data can be analyzed in order to determine what solution is the best one for this specific issue. Sometimes you need to modify your hypothesis and procedure then try again. That is OK though! Science is a series of trials which help us develop deeper understanding.

1. What needs to be done before you can propose a solution to a problem?

   A. Develop a hypothesis
   B. Create a procedure
   C. Identify a problem
   D. Analyze data

2. The Scientific Method is best described as

   A. A bunch of trials about different things
   B. An organized, step-by-step process
   C. A new product
   D. A hypothesis

3. If you do not find the right solution to your issue, what should you do?

   A. Give up
   B. Find a different problem to solve
   C. Make up data
   D. Modify your procedure and try again

Yesterday, you learned about the relationship between developing a solution and the Scientific Method. Today you will explore some examples of this process with some hands-on activities.

Directions: Read each text below and analyze for a solution. Then answer the question that follows.

Sprinkles, Sprinkles Everywhere

A company that sells rainbow sprinkles is trying to make the container they sell the sprinkles in better for the consumer. Right now they have a tall cylindrical bottle that is open at the top. Their customers have complained that because the top is so wide open, sprinkles spill out easily when they are trying to decorate their baked goods.

1. What problem that customers have identified?

2. What is a design solution that could help solve this problem?

Observations In Nature

If you look out your window, you might spot a bird or two. Even if you can't see them, though, you might hear them. Birds make a lot of different calls and songs. Each species of bird has their own set of vocalizations.

3. What is the phenomenon here that you are observing?

4. If you wanted to learn about the calls of one species of bird, what process might you do in order to figure it out?

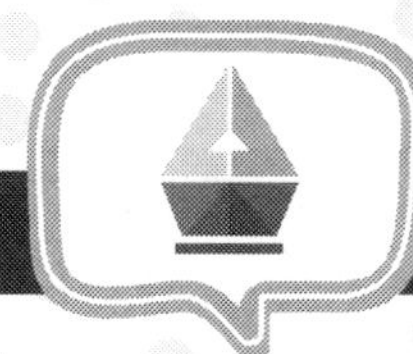

Competing Solutions

Let's pretend you are the head of a pharmaceutical company and you have two scientists who have developed a medicine for the common cold. Both of them claim their medicine works faster than the other scientist's medicine.

5. How could you go about comparing the effectiveness of these two different medicines?

Yesterday, you explored various issues and products and identified how to develop or test solutions to them. Today you will explain these solutions in more detail.

Directions: Read each text below. Then answer the questions that follow.

Sprinkles, Sprinkles Everywhere

You identified that a sprinkles container needs to be redesigned so that sprinkles do not easily spill out of it.

1. How could you test that your redesign worked? How would you know you've found a good solution to this problem?

Observations In Nature

You identified a procedure for determining what the calls of one species of bird mean.

2. What is difficult about proposing hypotheses about living creatures and their behavior?

Competing Solutions

You identified that it would be important to test two medications designed to quickly alleviate the common cold in order to determine which one was more effective.

3. If both medicines were equally effective, what might be the next step?

Week 17 Creating A Solution

Day 4 EXPERIMENTING WITH THE TOPIC

Yesterday you explained how to create and test solutions to issues and problems. This also allowed you to think about the Scientific Process in a bit more detail. Today you will experiment with creating a solution to a problem in your own home based on a procedure that you design in order to test your hypothesis.

Background:

When you wash cotton fabric and then dry it, it often comes out wrinkled. You hypothesize that it might have something to do with the type of soap being used.

Materials:

1. An item of clothing or a piece of fabric made of 100% cotton
2. 4 different kinds of soap (laundry detergent, dish soap, hand soap, bodywash, etc)
3. A large bowl or basin
4. Warm water
5. A dryer or a clothesline
6. A pencil and paper to record data

Follow-Up Questions:

1. What is the problem you are trying to find a solution to?

2. What do you think a possible solution is?

3. What are you testing?

4. How are you going to test it? For this question, develop a process for testing your hypothesis.

....

....

....

....

5. What data will you record from this process?

....

....

....

....

6. What soap produced the least number of wrinkles?

....

....

....

....

Week 17  Creating A Solution

Day 5 ELABORATING ON THE TOPIC

Yesterday, you designed an experiment to test what soap type causes more or less wrinkles in cotton fabric. Today you will elaborate on this experiment and further explain how this process helps create good solutions to issues.

Directions: Read and answer each question below.

1. Why do you think the soap type that produced the least number of wrinkles proved to be the best solution?

2. Why did you want to test more than one soap type?

3. What is important to keep the same between trials? For example, we used the same cotton fabric with each trial - what else might you want to keep constant?

4. If all of the soap types produced the same amount of wrinkles, what might you conclude?

5. Why is it important to test a soap type more than once if you can?

6. Do you think it is important to test solutions before using them?

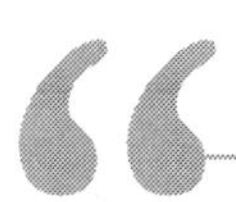

Engineering

Testing Ideas

MS-ETS1-4

Develop a step-by-step process to test your model/idea and gather data about its effectiveness.

Week 18 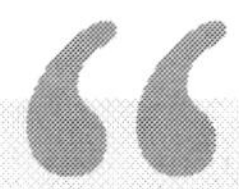 Testing Idea

Day 1 ENGAGING WITH THE TOPIC

Directions: Read the text below. Then answer the questions that follow.

Testing An Idea

Last lesson you explored how to design a solution to a problem. Today you will explore in more detail how you would test your ideas or solutions. We began to explore how you might test solutions in order to determine which one is the best for a specific issue. In the Scientific Method, this process of testing is called a procedure. A procedure is an organized, step-by-step process that is designed to allow you to collect data about solutions you are testing.

It is important that your **procedure** be designed so that you know you are testing only one thing. For this we have what are called dependent and independent variables. The **independent variable** is related to the thing you change. The **dependent variable** is what you measure - you would expect to see it change because it depends on the independent variable. For example, if you wanted to test favorite ice cream flavor in a group of people, the independent variable wouldbe ice cream flavor and the dependent variable would be each person's response as to how much they liked that flavor.

You also want **constants** when testing an idea. These are things you keep the same so that you know you are only changing the independent variable. For example, if I tested different ice cream flavors in a group of people, but I added different toppings to each one as well,it would be hard to determine if the people were responding to the ice cream flavor or the toppings. You only want to test one variable at a time - therefore everything else should stay constant.

1. In an experiment, does the independent variable change?

   A. Yes, the experimenter changes it for each trial
   B. Yes, the test subject changes it
   C. Yes, the independent variable will change in response to the dependent variable
   D. No

2. You would associate the data you collected with what aspect of a procedure?

   A. Independent variable
   B. Dependent variable
   C. Hypothesis
   D. Constants

3. True or False: It is good to change more than one variable data time.

   A. True
   B. False

Yesterday, you learned how to design a good test for an idea.Today you will try to identify key aspects of a great experimental design in the following examples.

Directions: Read each text below and analyze for a solution. Then answer the question that follows.

A Picky Eater

You have a hunch that your pet cat prefers wet food over dry food because she seems to eat more when you feed her wet food. You buy 4 different brands of cat food, two wet and two dry. You feed her at ½ a cup of food the same time every day and rotate between the 4 brands of food over a two week timespan. By the end of it you have tested each food at least 4 times.

1. What is the independent variable?

2. What is the dependent variable?

Better Sleep

You've read online that certain smells can help a person sleep better. You buy a few air fresheners for your room to test this. You get one lavender, one peach and one pine scented air freshener. You place each one in your room for 3 consecutive days and record about how many hours of sleep you get each night.

3. What things would you want to keep constant in this experiment?

Keep That Bug Away!

Is mosquito season and you want to keep them as far away from you as possible. You've heard of some natural remedies for mosquito repellant and want to test which one is most effective at deterring mosquito bites on your family members.

4. What is the independent variable in this experiment?

5. What things should the experimenter keep constant?

Yesterday, you identified some key components of good experimental design. Today you will further analyze these hypothetical experiments and explain how to test an idea in more detail.

Directions: : Read each text below. Then answer the questions that follow.

A Picky Eater

You identified that in this experiment, the type of cat food was the independent variable and the amount that was eaten by the cat was the dependent variable.

1. Why was it important to test both dry and wet cat food?

2. What is one thing that might be hard to control or keep constant in an experiment with a live animal?

Better Sleep

You identified a number of things you would want to keep constant in an experiment about how smell impacts the quality of sleep.

3. If there was no difference in the average amount of sleep you got with any of the scents, what would this mean?

Keep That Bug Away!

You identified it would be important to test two medications designed to quickly alleviate the common cold in order to determine which one was more effective.

4. What could be the dependent variable in this experiment?

5. Why is it important to test the repellants on multiple people?

Week 18 Testing Idea

Day 4 EXPERIMENTING WITH THE TOPIC

Yesterday you explained some of the pros and cons to various procedures for testing ideas. Today you will design your own experiment to test a particular hypothesis about a natural phenomenon.

Background:

You've noticed that when you place tap water in your ice cube tray it takes longer to freeze than when you use filtered water. You want to test this idea and see if the type of water impacts how long it takes for that water to freeze into solid ice cubes. If you have the materials at home, please do conduct the experiment that you design.

Materials:

1. Tap water
2. Filtered water
3. Distilled water
4. Spring water
5. 4 identical ice cube trays
6. A watch or a timer

Follow-Up Questions:

1. What is your hypothesis?

2. Write a brief experiment you could conduct to test your hypothesis.

3. In this experiment, what is your independent variable?

4. In this experiment, what is your dependent variable?

5. What should you keep constant?

Yesterday, you designed an experiment to test if different types of water freeze into solid ice cubes faster than other types of water. Today you will elaborate on and refine how to test this idea.

Directions: Read and answer each question below.

1. What is one reason that filtered water might freeze faster than tap water?

2. Why do you want to use the same ice cube tray for each water type?

3. If there is no difference in freezing time between water types, what does this mean?

4. Why might you want to test each water type more than once?

5. Why would it be helpful to know how long it takes for different water types to freeze? Think of a profession or field of work this might impact. Or perhaps an aspect of the natural world.

WEEK 19

Engineering

Analyzing Test Results

MS-ETS1-3

Analyze the data from testing and determine how it can be used to improve upon the original design idea.

Directions: Read the text below. Then answer the questions that follow.

How To Analyze Data For An Experiment

So far we have discussed the importance of identifying problems, proposing hypotheses, and then testing your ideas. Today we will explore ways to analyze data from an experiment. **Data** is the information you record when you complete a trial or an experiment, and in most instances is the dependent variable.

There are two kinds of data. The first kind of data is **quantitative** data. This is data that is reported in numbers or quantity. Quantitative data can be used to find averages and other types of patterns. Some examples of quantitative data might include the number of people with brown hair, the temperature of an environment every day or the height of a building. All of these are reported in numbers and specific units. Quantitative data is easy to visually display this information in tables and graphs.

The other type of data is **qualitative data.** This is data that describes the quality of something - think adjectives! Some examples of qualitative data might be the color of an animal's fur, the smell of a species of flower species of flowers or the sounds birds make when they are communicating. Qualitative data can be used to create a narrative or a description of a phenomenon.

1. Which type of data is usually reported with numbers?

   A. Narrative
   B. Dependent variable
   C. Qualitative
   D. Quantitative

2. Temperature would fall into the category of ______ data.

   A. Narrative
   B. Dependent variable
   C. Qualitative
   D. Quantitative

3. Which of the following would be qualitative data?

   A. The weight of a polar bear
   B. The size of a family of mongoose
   C. The texture of peacock feathers
   D. The number of teeth a white shark has

Yesterday, you learned about quantitative and qualitative data. Today you will read about different experiments and explore the different ways that data can be analyzed.

Directions: Read each text below and analyze. Then answer the question that follows.

Preferences In Female Rabbits

There is a population of rabbits that contain males that are either brown or black in fur color. Females will choose mates to have offspring with in the early spring. An experiment is conducted in order to determine if females choose to mate with male rabbits based on the color of their fur.

1. Is fur color quantitative or qualitative?

2. If females were choosing one color or fur over the other color of fur when it came to mating, how would you know? What data would you record?

Getting Rid Of Allergies

A scientist has developed a new medicine for easing the symptoms of seasonal allergies. The scientist claims the medicine lowers the symptom of sneezing, particularly when a person comes into contact with either pollen or dust.

3. What data would you want to record if you were testing this medicine?

4. How would you know if it did ease symptoms for people with allergies?

It's All About Color

A naturalist notices that fireflies tend to be attracted to light sources. She wants to know if the color of the light affects how attracted they are to the light. She buys a blue light, a red light and a white light and places them in different parts of a field at night and then records the fireflies' behavior.

5. Since the naturalist cannot ask the fireflies which light they prefer,how might she measure how attracted they are to a color of light?

6. Based on your answer to question #5, is this a quantitative or qualitative form of data?

Yesterday, you identified different kinds of data in different experiments. Today you will further consider and explain how that data could be analyzed and interpreted.

Directions: Read each text below. Then answer the questions that follow.

Preferences In Female Rabbits

You identified that recording the number of matings or number of offspring could help you determine if female rabbits had a preference for fur color in male rabbits. Below is the data:

	Males with Black Fur	Males with Brown Fur
Number of Offspring	392	583

1. Which fur color is more attractive to female rabbits based on this data?

2. What else would you want to know about this population of rabbits in order to make sure you can with certainty say preference is correlated to fur color?

Getting Rid Of Allergies

You identified that in order to measure the effectiveness of a new allergy medication, you'd want to analyze the symptoms of people taking it.

3. If the sneezes became milder for both people with allergies and people without allergies who had taken the medication, what conclusion would you draw?

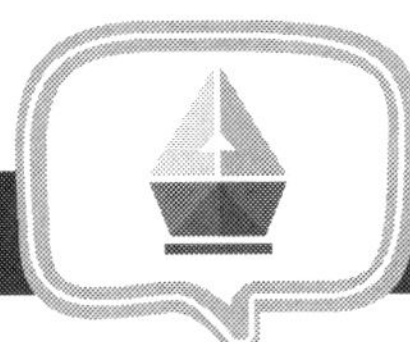

It's All About Color

You concluded that quantitative data about proximity to or time spent around a certain color of light could be used to determine if fireflies prefer certain color lights over others. The data below shows:

	Blue	Red	White
Average Time Fireflies Spent Touching Light	5.6 minutes	6.7 minutes	5.2 minutes

4. What would you want to have as a constant in this experiment?

5. What light is most attractive to fireflies based on this data?

Yesterday you explained analyzed data from some hypothetical tests and experiments. You also elaborated on data and how to refine these experiments. Today you will analyze data from an experiment.

Background:

A local birdwatcher is trying to determine population counts for a few bird species throughout the year. Every day she goes to the same spot in the local park and records every cardinal, chickadee, and Canadian geese she sees. Every month she adds up her counts. Below is the data in a table and in a bar graph.

Month	Cardinal	Chickadee	Canadian Geese
April	291	475	71
May	290	488	75
June	294	520	82
July	292	531	81
August	283	527	83
September	256	521	61
October	278	524	42
November	203	538	33
December	201	526	17
January	189	522	12
February	212	499	29
March	256	408	44

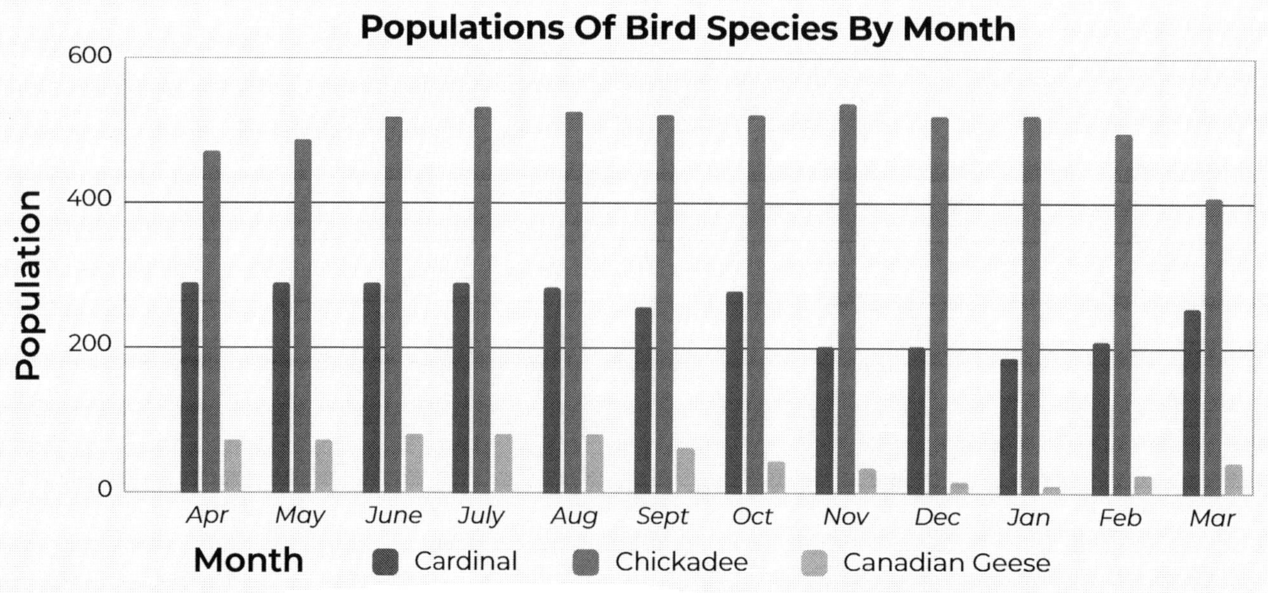

Questions

1. What population was the largest throughout the year?

2. Which population was the smallest in January?

3. Which population changed the most throughout the year?

4. Between February and March, what happened to the cardinal population?

5. Between October and November, what happened to the chickadee population?

6. What was the population for the Canadian geese in June?

ELABORATING ON THE TOPIC

Yesterday, you analyzed data from a study on bird populations. Today you will elaborate on these findings and draw further conclusions about what it means to analyze data.

Directions: Read and answer each question below.

1. When looking up the specific population for a bird species, was it easier to determine it from the table or the bar graph?

2. Are population counts quantitative or qualitative?

3. What is one issue with reporting total numbers of birds in a month? Do you see any issues with how the scientist collected her data?

4. Based on the monthly bird counts for Canadian geese, what can you infer?

5. Which population do you think is most consistent throughout the year? Why do you believe that?

6. In general, was it easier to make comparisons between bird species based on the numbers on the table or the bar graph? Why? This is an opinion-based question - there is no right answer.

WEEK 20

Engineering

Editing Ideas & Designs

MS-ETS1-4

Re-design original idea and expand on the idea that editing ideas is an important part of the process.

Directions: Read the text below. Then answer the questions that follow.

How & When To Edit An Idea Or Design

Now that you know how to analyze data, you can begin to think about how we use that information when editing an idea or a design. Editing is one of the most important parts of science and engineering. Editing is what allows us to challenge our understanding of the natural world and dig deeper into problems.

Let's take an example. Prosthetic limbs used to be made from very heavy materials such as wood and metal. They were sturdy but hard to maneuver and weren't always the right shape for a patient. Over time, people tried to tackle these issues and redesign prosthetic limbs so that they were made of lighter materials and shapes to fit different body types. None of this would have been possible if original designs and ideas weren't edited and improved as we learned more about materials and human anatomy.

When editing an idea or design it is crucial that you consider data. Just trying a new idea without supporting it with data or some sort of reason is not advisable. Having a reason for making a change ensures that you are addressing a specific issue for an identifiable reason.

1. What are the benefits of editing an idea?

   A. Improved design of a product
   B. Better understanding of the natural world
   C. Allows for more people to be helped
   D. All Of the above

2. What was one improvement made to prosthetic limbs?

   A. They were made of wood
   B. They came in only one shape
   C. They were made of lighter materials
   D. They cost less

3. When is it good to edit an idea?

   A. When you have data to support a change
   B. When something works really well
   C. When you have identified a problem but have not yet tested it
   D. Any time you want to

Yesterday, you learned about the importance of editing ideas and why new ideas and designs should be backed by data. Today you will explore some hypothetical examples and identify new ideas or designs.

Directions: Read each text below and analyze. Then answer the question that follows.

When Do People Shop?

A store owner has noticed that his store seems really empty for the last hour it is open, between 6pm and 7pm. He wants to determine if he should shorten the hours his store is open and close at 6pm instead of 7pm.

1. What data is the store owner using to support his idea?

2. If his store is no emptier at 6pm then at 7pm right before closing, what does this mean?

More Insects Everywhere

A scientist is seeing an increase in the population of locust across the world. She compiles population counts and compares it with hectares of agricultural land that are being lost to locust feeding on crops planted by farmers.

	Taiwan	South Africa	Chili
Locust Population	290,030,380	198,940,189	501,938,732
Farmland Lost (in hectares)	1,670	1,720	2,930

3. What issue is the scientist concerned with in her study?

4. What conclusion can you draw from this data?

Making A Faster Shoe

A sneaker designer has tested a new sole that is made of synthetic rubber. He has found that runners can run 10% faster when wearing sneakers with this sole compared to vulcanized rubber soles. This sneaker costs about 25% more to produce.

5. What part of the sneaker was redesigned?

Yesterday, you identified how different issues or products might be redesigned after data is collected. Today you will explain in more detail how editing an idea or design works.

Directions: Read each text below. Then answer the questions that follow.

When Do People Shop?

You determined that a store owner needs to count the number of shoppers in his store at different times of the day in order to determine if he can change his store hours.

1. Why would it be bad for the shop owner to change his hours without collecting data first?

2. Why might the shop owner want to collect data for multiple days or weeks instead of just one day?

More Insects Everywhere

You identified that an increase in the populations of locust is causing agricultural land to be lost.

3. What solution might be proposed to solve this issue?

4. If the solution you proposed in question #4 does not improve things for farmers, what would you do next?

Making A Faster Shoe

You learned that a new shoe design makes runners 10% faster and also cost 25% more to produce.

5. What is one drawback to this new show design?

6. How might you edit your design to make improvements in terms of price?

Yesterday you explained how the conclusions drawn from data could be interpreted and used to edit an idea or a design. Today you will analyze and continue that work in more depth with a product redesign.

Background:

A new blood sugar monitor has been developed by a team of researchers. Blood sugar monitors are used by individuals with diabetes so they can keep their blood sugar within a healthy range. This blood sugar monitor connects with a smartphone and records blood sugar levels every two hours. Below is some feedback from diabetics who used this monitor in a trial.

Feedback:

Patient	Age	Feedback
A	32	Pump is easy to wear clothes over. I particularly like the feature that it notifies my doctor if my blood sugar levels dip extremely low.
B	24	It functions similar to the current model of blood sugar monitor I use but it is smaller. I wish I could set it so that it montors my blood sugar every hour.
C	29	It is easy to navigate the app and it makes communication with my doctor very simple - I used to have to send my numbers in a spreadsheet once a week to my doctor. I like how easily it is to wear because it is smaller than other monitors.
D	57	I liked my old monitor better because I could set it to monitor my blood sugar level every 30 minutes. This one is also hard to read because it is so small.
E	31	I like that this monitor displays and saves my blood sugar levels in the app. I have been contacted by my doctors twice when my levels drop low at night when I am sleeping which has been very helpful.
F	25	I have worn this blood sugar monitor under all types of clothes very comfortably.

Questions

1. What was one issue patient C had with their old model of blood sugar monitor?

2. Is the data from this trial quantitative or qualitative?

3. What is the redesign feature that most people commented positively about?

4. What patient needs to monitor their blood sugar levels every thirty minutes?

5. Who uses the data collected by the blood sugar monitor?

6. In order to use this blood sugar monitor, what other piece of technology must you own?

Week 20 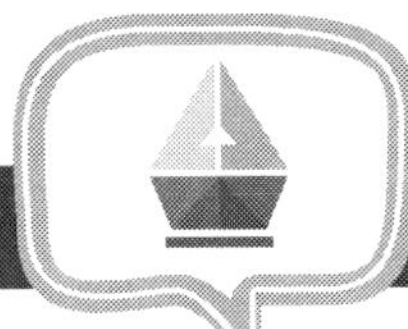 Editing Ideas & Designs

Day 5 ELABORATING ON THE TOPIC

Yesterday, you analyzed feedback from diabetic patients in a trial for a new blood sugar monitor. Today you will elaborate on your analysis of data and propose new ideas for design.

Directions: Read and answer each question below.

1. Based on the design of the blood sugar monitor and the feedback, what is one issue you believe the researchers were trying to address in this model?

2. What is one benefit of the blood sugar monitor's small size? What is one drawback of the blood sugar monitor's small size?

3. What aspect of the blood sugar people do multiple people want more control over?

4. What is one drawback to the fact that you must have a smartphone in order to be able to use this blood sugar monitor?

5. If you were going to redesign this new blood sugar monitor, based on all of the feedback, what would you choose to redesign?

6. If you change anything about the design of this blood sugar monitor, do you think you have to complete another trial?

ANSWER KEYS

Answer Key

Week 1

Day 1

1. A & B
2. C
3. B

Day 2

1. Answers will vary. Most likely the most common types will be cotton, rayon and polyester.
2. Yes
3. Yes
4. No
5. No

Day 3

1. Answers will vary.
2. Cotton is absorbent so it would be good in something like a towel or something that needs to wick moisture away from skin. It would not be good for a garment that you don't want to wrinkle or if you hate ironing! Answers will vary.
3. Polyester would be a terrible fiber for a sponge or mob. It is great for clothing that you do not want to wrinkle - you could throw it into a suitcase or a drawer and not worry! Answers will vary.

Day 4

1. Answers will vary, but in general the natural fibers will tear easier, stretch less, be more absorbent and stain easily when pigment is placed on them. In general synthetic fibers will not tear easily, stretch more, are less absorbent and do not stain easily when pigment is placed on them.

Day 5

1. Natural fibers tear easier, stretch less, be more absorbent and stain easily when pigment is placed on them.
2. Synthetic fibers will not tear easily, stretch more, are less absorbent and do not stain easily when pigment is placed on them.
3. Answers will vary. Natural fibers can be quite durable and are eco-friendly. Synthetic fibers are cheaper and stain-resistant.
4. Humans need fabrics for different types of products and needs. Synthetics allow humans to use chemical equations to create fabrics with the exact properties they need for a given reason.
5. Answers will vary but may include:

A. Stretch for easy movement

B. Easy to dye so jersey can be dyed team's colors

C. Non-absorbent so sweat can evaporate while players are exercising

Answer Key

Week 2

Day 1

1. C
2. C
3. D

Day 2

1. Liquid water
2. The food coloring moves faster and mixes in more quickly in the glass of hot water.
3. The water in the it's no longer glass wrapped in aluminum is warmer.

Day 3

1. Ice has almost no thermal energy which means the molecules are not moving around. This is why it is solid. Liquid water has more thermal energy and the molecules are there free to move and slosh around in the plate.
2. Boil water requires more thermal energy. If you boil water and it turns to steam, the water molecules in the steam are moving even faster than the water molecules in liquid water.
3. As you add thermal energy to water, the molecules are carrying the food coloring around the glass more quickly than in the cold water.
4. Aluminum seems to help keep thermal energy in the glass of water, a process known as insulation. The energy thermal does not escape into the surrounding environment as quickly.

Day 4

1. Results will vary depending on the insulating materials chosen.
2. The cup without insulation will have the most amount of ice in it or perhaps be frozen solid completely.
3. Result will vary but usually materials that are thicker or have air trapped in them (such as with bubble wrap) will insulate best and result in little to no ice being formed.
4. The cup without insulation should have the lowest temperature.
5. One of the insulated cups should have the highest temperature.

Day 5

1. They had the least amount of thermal energy (heat) and therefore the water molecules slowed down so much that the water became solid or frozen.
2. Insulating materials help trap or maintain thermal energy.
3. When water is insulated, the movement of water molecules changes less than if water is not insulated. This is because thermal energy is maintained in the glass.
4. If insulation was removed, thermal energy would be lost from the water more quickly. It would therefore change state faster and go from being a liquid to a solid more quickly.
5. You would want a lunchbox to be insulated so that cold food stayed cold and hot food stayed hot. Thicker materials or materials like metal such as aluminum seem to be great insulators and help regulate how much thermal energy is inside a container such as a lunchbox.

Week 3

Day 1

1. B
2. C
3. C

Day 2

1. No
2. No, barely at all if any change occurs.
3. The weight stayed almost exactly the same.

Day 3

1. Since there isn't a reaction, just a physical change, there should not be a change in the weight of the water, cup and sugar when added together.
2. The weight did not change because the reaction produced popped popcorn and some steam in the closed environment (i.e. the microwave popcorn bag). Popcorn kernels are more dense and when you pop them, they become less dense and release water vapor as a byproduct.
3. Similar to the previous demonstration, baking soda and vinegar cause a reaction which releases gas and a vigorous chemical reaction. The weight does not change from start to finish however as all products of the reaction are trapped in the plastic soda bottle, including the gas.

Answer Key

Day 4

1. Combustion
2. The wood
3. The ashes
4. They are both solid (wood and ashes)
5. The sum of the wood and the fire is 11lbs and the sum of the ashes and the smoke is also 11 lbs. They are equal in mass!
6. The weight of the ashes and the smoke would also increase because matter is never destroyed (one of the parts of the Law Of Conservation Of Mass)

Day 5

1. No, they are just recombined into something new. For example, when wood burns it becomes smoke and ashes.
2. No, as as was stated day #4, smoke has weight. Smoke is mostly gases. As we saw on day #2, water also has mass and it is a liquid.
3. It would mean that either:

   A. Your reaction did not take place in a closed container so some of the products of the reaction were lost.

   B. You did not weigh one of the products because you did not realize it was formed from the reaction (for example, water vapor is hard to capture and you may not be able to easily weigh it weight).
4. No, the rust has a weight and the remaining iron has weight according to the Law Of Conservation Of Mass. Those two types of matter added together should have the same mass as the original fence (plus a little oxygen which oxidizes or is used in the chemical reaction of the rusting of a fence).
5. The weight of the cake should be the same as the weight of all of the individual ingredients used to make it. Based on the Law Of Conservation Of Mass, the atoms are just rearranged from the ingredients to make the cake - no atoms are made or destroyed.

Answer Key

Week 4

Day 1

1. D
2. B
3. C

Day 2

1. Air moving out of the balloon.
2. The heavier object - the more force it puts on the scale, the higher the weight reads on the scale.
3. The heavier object.
4. No, it doesn't bounce straight back at you. There is always a slight change in the angle at the very lease.

Day 3

1. The air being released is moving backwards behind the balloon which in turn pushes the balloon forward in the opposite direction but with equal force.
2. The heavier object exerts more force on your arm - that is why it is harder to lift it up.
3. When you do a bicep curl, your arm is exerting force against the weight in order to lift it up. The weight is in turn pressing down on your arm with equal and opposite force. You could also argue that gravity is exerting equal force downwards on both the weight/object and your arm.
4. The direction your arm pushes on the ball as it rolls it forward changes, at least slightly, each time you roll the ball. This means when the ball meets the wall and exerts force on the wall, the wall pushes back with an equal and opposite force, showing you the pathway the ball traveled to get to the wall (but opposite). The reflection of the movement shows you the change in movement your arm and the ball had on each other.

Answer Key

Day 4

1. When a bird flaps its wings it pushes down on the surrounding air. The air in turn pushes up on the bird's wings with opposite and equal force. This keeps the bird up in the air.
2. Answers will vary.
3. Answers will vary.
4. Generally birds that have smaller wingspans need to flap their wings more in order to stay airborne. Birds with very large wingspans, such as birds of prey, can glide and flat less often.
5. Birds will change the direction their wings are pointing, the angle of their body, the way their head is pointed and more in order to change direction during flight. This places the force of the air on different points of contact with their body and allows them to turn.

Day 5

1. The wings pushing downward on the air and the air pushing upward on the wings of the bird.
2. The bird is gliding. This means that the force of the air under their wings is enough to keep the weight of the bird in the air without the need for added force from the wings flapping.
3. Answers will vary but birds generally flap less often and change the direction their wings are pointed. They minimize the amount of force they are exerting on the surrounding air. They rarely just close their wings together because they would fall to the Earth without much control. Using some light force from their wing on the air helps them land safely.
4. Birds with shorter wingspans generally need to flap more often since they exert less force on the air with each flap.
5. Answers will vary. You may choose to "design" a bird with a larger wingspan, a lighter body, stronger muscles, etc. You choose a characteristic that allows the bird to exert more force on the surrounding area so that it needs to flap less often.

Answer Key

Week 5

Day 1

1. D
2. B
3. A

Day 2

1. A rainbow of colors! If done well, you can see red, blue, orange, yellow, blue, green and purple.
2. Shiny things reflect images and light.
3. The reflection of a face changes. On the back of the spoon, the image looks stretched out. One the front of the spoon the image looks squished together. Now you understand why mirrors are completely flat - this gives the most accurate reflection without distorting it.
4. The light disappears and it looks black/ you cannot see what is on the other side of the two overlapping pairs of sunglasses. This is because of the polarized lenses.

Day 3

1. Light cannot penetrate (or move through) substances that are too thick. A mist breaks up the water molecules into a thin layer, making it easy for light to move through the water. Also, depending on where the light hits, it slows down the wavelength of light more or less, causing different colors to appear.
2. Light moves as a cyclical pattern. If it bounces off surfaces that are different angles and distances from the eye, it will affect the overall image. It causes images to look warped or distorted.
3. Sunglasses have polarized lenses. These lenses are made to block out some wavelengths of light. Think of it like a shade on a window with parallel slats. When you overlap these lenses, the slats line up and some light can still get through. When you turn the lenses, the slats no longer overlap and all the light is blocked.

Answer Key

Day 4

1. You want to make sure the thermometers are both working and start at the same temperature when you begin your experiment.
2. Results can vary but it should be the one under the white piece of paper.
3. Results can vary but it should be the one under the black piece of paper.
4. Results can vary but it should be the black paper.
5. Black objects absorb all wavelengths of light. White objects reflect all wavelengths of light.
6. Light is made of magnetic fields as well as electric fields. We learned about the relationship between energy and thermal heat in a previous week's lesson.

Day 5

1. Light is made up of energy. If something absorbs light energy, it can be converted to thermal energy.
2. Black objects absorb all wavelengths of light so they absorb energy. This energy becomes thermal heat, causing the temperature to rise.
3. Asphalt is black or dark in color so it absorbs sunlight. This is why the temperature of the asphalt can be much hotter than the air around it.
4. White becauce white reflects all colors of light. This means it does not absorb energy.
5. Both white paper and the shiny spoon reflect at least some wavelength of light.

Answer Key

Week 6

Day 1

1. D
2. C
3. A

Day 2

1. Results will vary.
2. In most instances totals for the cold hands should be lower than totals for the warm hands.
3. Results can vary but in general your palm should have been most accurate in differentiating between the number of pencil pokes and the other two parts of the body should be less accurate.

Day 3

1. Information needs to be picked up by your sense of sight, brought to your brain for processing, and then the decision to catch the ruler needs to be sent to your hand. This all takes a number of milliseconds to complete.
2. In order for your sense of touch to work properly, you need to be able to feel what you are touching. Cold slows down the neurons in your hands making it harder to control them with your brain. This slows down the processing of your nervous system and therefore makes it harder for you to pick up pennies as fast as you were able to with warm hands.
3. We use our hands to manipulate the world around us all the time. We therefore have way more touch receptors or touch neurons on our hands. There are very few neurons on the back of our arms and neck because we don't take touch information in from these parts of the body as regularly. The hand is most accurate when it comes to touch because there are more neurons in our hands that are sensitive to this type of information.

Answer Key

Day 4

1. Results will vary
2. Results will vary but this is usually the toughest trial.
3. Result will vary but this is usually the easiest trial.
4. Foods that look unique or have very strong smells tend to be easiest to remember. Also the first food and the last food in the lineup are easiest to remember in general.
5. Foods that do not look unique, do not smell strong, or smell similar to other things are hardest to remember. Foods in the middle of the lineup are hardest to remember and are easy to mix up.
6. Harder because they probably all have similar smells or even perhaps similar looks.

Day 5

1. The sensory neurons in your eyes pick up sight information and bring it from the PNS to the CNS where your brain processes that information. A memory of the order of food is then created by the brain.
2. The sensory neurons in your nose pick up smell information and bring it from the PNS to the CNS where your brain processes that information. A memory of the order of food is then created by the brain.
3. Even though you are not receiving information from your senses when you are trying to remember the order of the food, your brain is accessing the memory of the pattern as best as it can. That memory is then translated back to yoru PNS in the form of words as you say the order of the food items.
4. There is more sensory input from the neurons in your PNS - input from two senses rather than just one.
5. Your brain captures and stores information you obtain from your senses so that you can access that same experience again in the future (a memory).
6. If a person is physically near the crime, they can see, smell, hear and use other senses to pick up on information. If they are down the block, they can probably only hear what is happening. A witness that is present at the crime would likely have a better memory of what happened because there was more information coming into their PNS through more sensory systems and therefore stronger memories are created by the CNS.

Answer Key

Week 7

Day 1

1. A
2. D
3. B

Day 2

1. Results will vary but the number of beans that can fit in the cup should be less after you add the marshmallows.
2. **A** because 1 marshmallow = 200lbs of food.
3. **B** because there is only 2000lb of food represented in this ecosystem but 2600lbs of food are needed to feed all of the animals represented by pennies and beans.
4. **B** because the wolves are eating the rabbits to feed their larger population.

Day 3

1. When humans build houses, we reduce the amount of space available for the populations of organisms in that ecosystem. This could cause that population to move to different ecosystems or the population could decline.
2. A population could:
   - **A.** Move to a new ecosystem
   - **B.** Start eating other types of food
   - **C.** Die off
3. If there are no rabbits, the wolves cannot eat so their population would begin to decrease.

Day 4

1. 2013
2. 2014
3. 2,390,819 in 2018
4. 2017
5. It was increasing
6. It increased

Answer Key

Day 5

1. As the temperature changes, so does the population of Prairie Coneflowers. Temperature is an abiotic, nonliving factor.
2. Yes, aphids and coneflower are both living, biotic factors. Since the aphids eat and kill coneflowers, the coneflowers responded with a decline in their population when the aphid population increased.
3. Since the coneflower population had decreased in 2018, there was not enough food to sustain the larger population of aphids. They likely began to die off as a result.
4. The coneflower population would increase since there would be no aphids around to eat and kill the coneflowers.
5. The population of coneflowers decreased in 2014 due to cold temperatures so if the temperatures were warmer than normal it might be plausible that the coneflower population would increase. Perhaps coneflowers do better in warmer weather. It is also possible that the coneflower population could decrease because 79 degrees might be too warm and this species of coneflower might only thrive in temperatures closer to the annual average of 75 degrees.

Week 8

Day 1

1. D
2. B
3. A

Day 2

1. Results will vary but you should be able to identify quite a lot of different species in a natural area that hasn't been impacted by humans very much.
2. Results will vary but it should have been harder to find much biodiversity in an area heavily developed by humans. This answer should be a lot lower than your answer to the previous question.
3. The rainforest will have the most biodiversity.
4. Either the desert or the tundra will have the lowest amount of biodiversity.

Day 3

1. There are lots of spaces for organisms to live - there aren't many buildings in these areas. If there is more space for plants, that means there is more space for food for and shelter animals. For example, a big field full of dozens of types of wildflowers is a great habitat for insects, birds, and even small mammals.
2. When humans create buildings, put in roads, and alter the natural landscape of an area, there is little space for plants to grow. This means there is less habitat, food, and shelter for animals. Chances are that any organisms you saw in a downtown area were placed there by humans.
3. Rainforests are warm, sunny and have lots of rainfall annually. This means plants can grow quickly and have lots of access to resources. With more plant life comes more animal life and diversity. Rainforests have the most biodiversity of any ecosystem on this planet.
4. Deserts and the tundra have very little rainfall and have very harsh environments. Since there is little space for shelter and other resources, not many living organisms can survive here easily.

Answer Key

Day 4

1. South Africa and Canada
2. South Africa
3. Oil, gas and tourism
4. About $500 million
5. Canada
6. Mining

Day 5

1. Canada is a very large country in terms of the amount of land it contains. Canada also has many different ecosystems so it may take more money to protect organisms in different habitats.
2. Answers will vary. Students may find that conservation is connected to hunting in South Africa. They might also find that conservation is also funded by a lot of nonprofit organizations in South Africa, not the government.
3. All of them! Mining disturbed the land above it, often causing pollution. Agriculture can lead to monocropping (when only one type of plant is grown) which causes farmers to lose biodiversity in their crops. Manufacturing can cause different forms of pollution which minimize biodiversity. Drilling or fracking for oil is bad for living creatures. Tourism is often dependent on natural beauty being preserved.
4. Answers will vary. Some considerations may include:
   - **A.** Cause a species to go extinct
   - **B.** Cause an invasive species to harm other species
   - **C.** Change the environment for organisms that survive off of another organism
5. New Zealand is a considerably smaller country in terms of landmass than Canada. Also New Zealand has less varity in the types of ecosystems it contains.

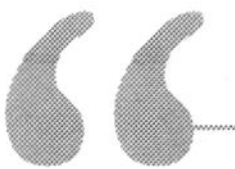

Answer Key

Week 9

Day 1

1. C
2. D
3. B

Day 2

1. Shape and color
2. These animals are pollinators and help with pollination amongst the orchid species they look like
3. No, if the organism begins to use its environment differently, it might not need a trait anymore. This makes that physical trait a vestigial structure.
4. No, some bacteria have different traits that allow them to be resistant to our antibiotics.

Day 3

1. Orchids that look like pollinators are more attractive. This means pollinators will visit them more frequently and help them spread their pollen. Pollen is how flowers reproduce. So in essence this relationship benefits the orchid because it allows them to reproduce more efficiently thanks to the help of the pollinators.
2. Answers will vary. Some students may say yes because there is no point in us making a structure we won't use. Other students may say no because if a wisdom tooth harms us in any way, it gets removed surgically - nothing is changing in our DNA to get rid of the structure. This is a debate that scientists are still having to this day.
3. Bacteria are single-celled and reproduce rapidly in ideal conditions such as the human body. Because of this, natural selection can allow for rapid evolution in bacteria populations, causing big changes in new strains. This means that if a bacteria comes into contact with an antibiotic, it could evolve resistance against it if it reproduces quickly enough and gains the right traits through natural selection.
4. Antibiotics are how we eradicate harmful bacteria from humans that have diseases. If a bacteria is resistant to all of our antibiotics, we have no way to help people get better.

Day 4

1. 10
2. The number of small salamanders increased.
3. The number of medium salamanders stayed relatively constant.
4. The number of large salamanders decreased.
5. The population of blue herons stayed relatively constant.
6. The area of the riverbed shrank over time.

Day 5

1. They were able to hide in the small pebbles of the riverbed best. They were able to hide from the blue herons better than the medium and large salamanders and therefore survived best. This means they were able to reproduce more over time, causing their population to increase.
2. The area of the riverbed decreased, making it harder for the salamanders to find places to hide from their predators.
3. The blue heron population stayed the same. Even though there weren't more predators, the amount of space where salamanders could hide was smaller which means the pressure of predation increased.
4. Overall the population will likely decrease if the riverbed continues to shrink. Overall, however, the small salamanders will survive best and the large salamanders might disappear all together.
5. No, it is not a fast process. In 30 years the populations only changed a little. Natural selection might occur with each generation but drastic changes in evolution could take hundreds, thousands or even millions of years. Consider human evolution - we haven't changed very much since our species of *Homo Sapiens* evolved over 200,000 years ago.

Answer Key

Week 10

Day 1

1. B
2. C
3. A

Day 2

1. Results will vary - many organic or natural products tend to be Non - GMO certified however.
2. A
3. C
4. A

Day 3

1. As discussed on day #1 of this week, GMOs can be used to do things such as extend the shelf life of food items. GMO foods can be altered so that they have traits that consumers prefer.
2. People who eat organic or natural food might not want organisms that are modified because it is considered "unnatural" - GMOs alter the normal DNA of an organism.
3. People can have allergic reactions to GMOs if the medicine is produced with organisms that a person reacts negatively to such as yeast.
4. Results will vary - we will look at this debate on day #4. This is an opinion based question but that opinion should be justified in some way.

Day 4

1. Monocropping (mono means one; crop is a harvest of food) will cause us to lose other species of rice. Monocropping is bad because it can cause the extinction of other species of similar organisms. Also, if the environment changed in a way that harmed Golden Rice and it all died, there would be no other species of rice to take its place.
2. Treating people who are developing blindness or have gone blind costs money. Preventing blindness saves money.
3. Vitamin A

Answer Key

4. When we ingest Golden Rice, its genome comes into contact with our own cells. We might not know if it impacts our body and physiology yet since this GMO is so new.
5. Environmental impact can be issues such as hazardous waste, toxins, pollution, or harming other plants and animals. If Golden Rice causes any of these issues, it could be more harmful overall than the initial concern of malnutrition.

Day 5

1. Neither. GMOs have negative and positive aspects to them just like many other solutions to world problems. Understanding the pros and cons is one of the most important things a scientifically-literate person can do.
2. Answers will vary. Examples from this lesson include helping with malnutrition, creating new medicines, helping minimize the spread of disease, creating shelf stable foods, etc.
3. Answers will vary. Examples from this lesson include unknown impacts on our GMO, negative environmental impacts, allergic reactions, monocropping, etc.
4. You need to know the entire genome of an organism. This means understanding all parts of its DNA and what DNA codes for what trait.
5. Answers will vary - perhaps a GMO spider that can spin steel-strength silk. Or maybe a sheep that grows 10X the normal amount of wool. Perhaps you engineer celery with fibers in it that can be woven into fabric. Let your imagination run wild! Make sure to consider the pros and cons of each idea, however.

Answer Key

Week 11

Day 1

1. C
2. A
3. C

Day 2

4. Answers will vary. If someone were 63 cm in height, you first need to see how many times 10cm goes into 63cm centimeters to find a conversion factor. Since 10 goes into 63 exactly 6.3 times, and 10cm in life = 1cm in your drawing, you then know you need to make your drawing 6.3 cm in height.
5. Answers will vary. If someone were 63 cm in height, then the conversion factor would be 63 divided by 10 which is 6.3 because 10 goes into 63cm 6.3 times. You would then take that conversion factor and multiple 100cm by 6.3 in order to determine that your image would be 630cm (or 6.3 meters) tall on the billboard.
6. Answers will vary. The process would be the same as you followed for question #1. If your room is 300cm wide, you would find how many times 10 goes into 300, which is 30 times. 30 multiplied by 1cm is 30cm. This means in yoru drawing you would need to draw your room with a width of 30 centimeters.

Day 3

1. First it was determined how many centimeters are represented by a single centimeter in the drawing. Then it was determined how many times that conversion fit into your actual height.
2. If you knew the diameter of a planet, you could divide that by a conversion factor that shrinks the diameter into a length that fits on a piece of paper.
3. Yes, tripling a recipe means you just take all of the measurements for ingredients and multiple them by 3. In this instance 3 is your conversion factor.
4. Since you know the distance between the Earth and the Sun is 150 million kilometers (or one Astronomical Unit, you could use the conversion factor from activity #1 to scale that distance down. First you could convert kilometers to meters and then divide by the conversion factor. In this case, you'd still need a HUGE piece of paper to draw that distance, so you'd need to scale down quite a bit more.

Answer Key

Day 4

Planet/Star	Distance in AU	Distance in cm (scaled down)
Sun	0.0 AU	0.0 cm
Mercury	0.4 AU	4 cm
Venus	0.7 AU	7 cm
Earth	1.0 AU	10 cm
Mars	1.5 AU	15 cm
Jupiter	5.2 AU	52 cm
Saturn	9.6 AU	96 cm
Uranus	19.2 AU	192 cm
Neptune	30 AU	300 cm
Pluto	39.5 AU	395 cm

1. AU are measured in distance between Earth and the sun - the sun cannot be any distance away from itself so that is why it is zero on either scale.
2. Venus
3. Venus and Earth, they are 0.3 AU apart or 3cm in your scale model.
4. Mars and Saturn are 8.1 AU apart or 81 cm apart in your scale model.

Day 5

1. The distance between planets is not equal and is different between each planet.
2. Empty space! There is a huge amount of distance between each planet.
3. Answers will vary. Some examples might be to use more accurate AU distances (more decimal places) or to use buttons and beads that are scaled down to be the right size for the planets they represent.
4. You would need a conversion factor that is larger. Instead of 1 AU = 1 cm as was the case in this demonstration, perhaps 1 AU = 1 meter.
5. If you know the distance from the telescope to the object it is taking an image of, you can use that to determine the conversion factor of that image.
6. Yes, as long as you knew what the conversion factor was that united the model and the actual spaceship it was built from. For example, if you measured the door on the spaceship to be 2cm high and knew that the door on the actual spaceship was 80cm high, you could determine the conversion factor between those two known measurements.

Answer Key

Week 12

Day 1

1. D
2. B
3. A

Day 2

1. Lava flowing from the volcano.
2. Answers will vary. Some observations might be that the volcano grows in size, it becomes wider and a bit flatter, it is irregular in shape, etc.
3. Answers will vary but it will likely take at least a couple rounds of shaking in order to unearth an object.
4. Answers will vary. The shape of the sand mound/ sandcastle will change even if it is subtle. It might get flatter, have little areas carved out by the water or areas of pooled water at the base of the sand mound. Sometimes as the sand gets wet large pieces will break off all of a sudden.

Day 3

1. If a volcano is really active, the lava can build up over time making larger volcanoes, mountains, or mountain ranges even. With each volcanic eruption the shape of the surrounding area will change depending on where the lava flows and how much lava is produced.
2. An earthquake.
3. If an earthquake occurred that was long enough, or multiple earthquakes occured in the same area over time, it could bring things like fossils to the surface of the Earth.
4. Rain.
5. If a mountain was subjected to a lot of rain for a long time, it could cause the mountain to erode or even disappear completely (although this could take millions of years).

Answer Key

Day 4

1. Difference layers of Earth. The lower layers formed a long time ago and the top layers are the most recently formed layers of Earth.
2. Layers form at different times and they don't really mix unless a major event happens such as an earthquake or a landslide.
3. Water from a stream, river or even an ocean. The Colorado River is what formed the Grand Canyon.
4. Rain
5. The inside of the canyon has the same layers of colored sand in the same order as what you can see from the outside of the box. The water carves into the Earth, revealing the layers that have formed over millions of years (or in the case of this lab, a couple minutes).

Day 5

1. Slow, steady processes. Canyons are carved out of solid Earth over millions of years of erosion caused by water.
2. If there is no water flowing, a canyon won't be formed. Drought could slow down the formation of a canyon.
3. It gets carried away by water - all freshwater eventually ends up in oceans so that eroded Earth (known as sediment) would end up in our oceans.
4. If there is more rainfall, more canyon could form or perhaps canyon form more quickly. If it is warmer in some areas, there might be more drought causing canyon formation to slow. Also drought can lead to what is known as wind erosion because soil becomes so dry it can blow away.
5. An Earthquake or a meteor hitting Earth's surface where there is a canyon.

Answer Key

Week 13

Day 1

1. D
2. D
3. A

Day 2

4. Water droplets collect on the underside of the plastic wrap.
5. A cloud forms in the bottle when a match is blown out and then added. A cloud did not form in the bottle when it was just shaken and then left alone.
6. The cup in the sun should have lost more water.

Day 3

1. Condensation - as the hot water evaporates (the steam coming off the surface of the water) it rises and then cools when it hits the ice.
2. The ice causes the condensation to occur more quickly so more water collects. Enough water might even collect where you see the water droplets falling back down into the bowl - this is precipitation.
3. Caused the water to become water vapor.
4. The smoke particles coming off of the match are warm and cause the water vapor to begin to condense around them. This forms a cloud. Clouds we see in the sky are water molecules condensing round dirt, pollution or other solid particles in our atmosphere.
5. Sunlight has a lot of energy, including thermal energy. Heat increases the temperature of the water and the water molecules begin to move faster and faster, increasing the speed at which they evaporate.

Day 4

1. Hawaii
2. Hawaii
3. Oregon
4. New Mexico
5. 10.91 inches
6. 40%

Day 5

1. Hawaii is an island so it is surrounded by water. Because of the warm temperatures and lots of sunshine, there is a ton of evaporation which leads to condensation and then precipitation in the form of rain.
2. Oregon's average temperature is above freezing - the Northwest area of the country is known for having a milder climate.
3. With more rainfall comes more water erosion - think back to the canyon lesson from the previous week. Also Hawaii is surrounded by ocean and coastlines are subjected to a lot of erosion by the ocean.
4. Good: warmer temperatures, some rainfall. Bad: some erosion and not as much rainfall as there could be.
5. Rainfall could increase since evaporation would speed up. Higher temperatures would likely mean less snowfall annually. This could also increase the amount of erosion which happens.

Week 14

Day 1

1. C
2. C
3. D

Day 2

1. Answers will vary. On average, Americans use between 80-100 gallons of water per a day!
2. The cup in the plastic bag will have warmer water.
3. The bowl under the dark blue paper should have warmer water.

Answer Key

Day 3

1. Water is used by all organisms. If we overuse water,it won't be available to wildlife, agriculture and freshwater sources might be depleted more quickly. Negatively impacting other organisms influences climate change.
2. Answers will vary. Some ideas include taking shorter showers, using water-efficient appliances, and washing clothes only when you need to.
3. If global water temperatures increase, this could be bad for aquatic organisms. Warming waters change organism's reproductive cycles, the availability of food and the currents in the ocean. Warm water also melts ice faster (see next question).
4. Ice is white and reflects the sun's rays, helping to cool the planet. If we lose our polar ice caps, our planet will warm even faster.

Day 4

1. 2019
2. 8 events in 1950 and 22 events in 1990.
3. 15 billion more tons of greenhouse gases.
4. Over 50,000 species have gone extinct.
5. The human population doubled.

Day 5

1. The number of people are increasing which is causing the amount of greenhouse gases to increase each year.
2. Species are going extinct at a much faster rate than in previous years - we have now lost an estimated 50,000 species and counting.
3. The planet has a finite number of resources and space - at some point the human population will grow to be so high that we do not have enough resources to support it.
4. As the global annual temperature increases, so too do the number of extreme weather events.
5. Temperatures would likely decrease and we would therefore lose less species and see fewer extreme weather events.

Answer Key

Week 15

Day 1

1. D
2. B
3. A

Day 2

1. Answers will vary. Some common answers will be heating the house, charging a phone or a laptop, powering a TV or video game system, cooking food, powering a car, lights in the home, etc.
2. Answers will vary. For most people it is food waste (either uneaten food or food wrappers).
3. Answers will vary. The average amount of garbage a person produces in a day is 5.5 lbs.
4. No, the pinto beans take up more space. Not all of the beans can fit because there is not enough graph squares available for all of them.

Day 3

1. Answers will vary. In home households the answer will be electricity.
2. Answers will vary. Some ideas include turning the lights off when you are not in a room, using energy-efficient appliances, having solar panels, only using items for a short amount of time every day, or not leaving items plugged in when you aren't using them.
3. Answers will vary. Recycling is a great option. Choosing to buy products that are packaged in biodegradable packaging is good too.
4. We are larger than many animals and take up more room between our homes, work space, schools and other businesses.
5. Eventually if there are too many beans, there won't be enough space for any individual to have the amount it needs. This could cause some animals and humans to be harmed or even go extinct.

Answer Key

Day 4

1. New Zealand
2. United States
3. 17%
4. New Zealand
5. It is an average for the entire country (it does not mean families contain fractions of a person).
6. 23% more

Day 5

1. Their homes are smaller.
2. Nonrenewable
3. Larger homes have more rooms, more lights, take more energy to heat and take more resources to build.
4. Solar and wind power.
5. The United States might end up producing less crude oil.
6. Their homes might get larger as would their average family size. This would lead to more energy usage and a bigger impact on the environment.

Answer Key

Week 16

Day 1

1. C
2. B
3. A

Day 2

1. Their harvests were declining.
2. The new housing development took the place of the wildflower field where all of the local pollinators used to live.
3. The bag rips when too much weight is placed in it.
4. The telescope is designed only for people who are right-handed, not left-handed.

Day 3

1. Perhaps a piece of land nearby could be converted into a new wildflower field to provide a new habitat for pollinators. People could also start planting gardens in the backyards of the houses in the new development to provide habitat for pollinators. If there are more pollinators, the farmer's harvests should improve.
2. Karen's bag could be made of a different material that can handle more weight - perhaps something thicker like canvas. Other Improvements include using stronger thread or using a different stitch to hold the bag pieces together.
3. The telescope could be designed so that the adjustment knobs were easily accessible regardless of what hand you were using - maybe have them placed in the middle instead of one side of the telescope.
4. If you only design for people with one type of ability, you minimize who has access to that product. Designing for all types of abilities means more people can use that product without experiencing issues. Equity through access is very important.

Answer Key

Day 4

1. Answers will vary.
2. Answers will vary.
3. Answers will vary. But more than likely it will be the mechanical pencil because of the shape of the lead - every time you click it for more lead, you get a point.
4. Answers will vary. Generally No.2 pencils are harder to erase because of the structure of their lead.
5. Answers will vary.
6. Pencils are not often designed for different handedness.

Day 5

1. Instead of redesigning something or addressing an issue without consideration, identifying the problem or the source of an issue helps guide you in figuring out what is more important to the people the issue/problem most affects. If there is no problem, there probably is no reason to try to change something.
2. Mechanical pencils don't need to be sharpened and can be reused - they were probably invented to negate the need for sharpening and reduce waste.
3. If you didn't have refills, mechanical pencils would be useless after they ran out of lead. Making them refillable makes them useful for longer and reduces waste.
4. Answers will vary.
5. You could add a grip that contours to a left-handed person holding the pencil, giving them more control or a better feel in their hand (ergonomic).
6. Answers will vary - perhaps making them out of recyclable materials or materials that are biodegradable.

Answer Key

Week 17

Day 1

1. C
2. B
3. D

Day 2

1. Sprinkles easily spill out of the container when they are decorating their baked goods.
2. Answers will vary. A top with holes big enough for some sprinkles to fall out of might slow spilling or make it easier to decorate with control.
3. Bird calls or bird songs.
4. Answers will vary. You would likely watch only birds of one species and record their calls. You could also want to make observations about their interactions and surroundings so you could draw conclusions about what each different call is possibly associated with. You would want to record calls a few times so as to make sure you have enough data to analyze. This is a very simplified procedure and you would want more detail in your actual process.
5. You would want to see how long it takes patients to recover with each individual medicine. You would want to test it on multiple subjects and record this data. Remember, the claim is that they help patients faster,so you want to focus on the speed of recovery.

Day 3

1. You would want multiple people to use the sprinkles container and report back if they experienced any spills. You would know if there was an improvement if you recorded data that there was less spilling compared with the original design of the sprinkle container.
2. Unlike the sprinkles container, you can't control a living organism without impacting its behavior. In order to observe and record data on a living organism, you have to watch it in its natural habitat and hope you hear it calling and notice everything about the environment in order to understand a phenomenon properly.
3. If both medicines were equally effective in terms of speed of recovery, you might ask the scientists to redesign the medicine using data that you collected from your original trials. Hopefully the data helps inform the scientist of what changes they might want to try in order to improve the effectiveness of the medicine.

Answer Key

Day 4

1. Wrinkled cotton fabric.
2. Changing the soap type used to wash the cotton fabric.
3. The difference in how much fabric wrinkles based on the type of soap used to wash it.
4. Hypothesis will vary. You will wash the same item of clothing in water and let it dry to see how much it wrinkles. You would want to complete this process at least once (but more trials is better) with each soap type.
5. The amount or number of wrinkles the fabric has after being washed with each soap type and then drying.
6. Answers will vary.

Day 5

1. Answers will vary. It will likely be the laundry detergent since it is specifically designed for fabrics.
2. If you only test one soap type, you have nothing to compare it to. Solutions can often come from surprising places and having more data is a great way to improve a possible solution.
3. Some good things to keep constant include the amount of water you are washing the fabric in, the temperature of the water, the bowl you are using, the method for drying, and the amount of time you let your fabric dry for etc.
4. That it was not the soap type that was leading to wrinkles.
5. The more trials you have, the better. If you only test once, you don't know if your results are something that occurs consistently or if they were an anomaly.
6. Answers will vary but yes, it is important.

Answer Key

Week 18

Day 1

1. A
2. B
3. B

Day 2

1. The type of cat food.
2. The amount of each type of cat food eaten by the cat.
3. Answers will vary. The time you go to bed, the time you wake up, the amount of exercise or activity you get each day, the amount of light in your room, the amount of noise in your bedroom, etc.
4. Type of natural remedy for mosquito repellent.
5. Answers will vary. Person they are testing on, amount of repellant used, amount of time spent outside, where the repellant is placed on the body, etc.

Day 3

1. If you only test wet food, you cannot compare it to your cat's preference for dry food - remember, your original hypothesis was that the cat liked wet food better than dry food.
2. Answers will vary. Controlling how hungry the cat is on any given day can be hard to manage, especially if the cat's activity level differs a lot from day to day.
3. That scent has no impact on sleep quality - or at least not these particular scents. You might want to test other scents to be more sure.
4. Number of mosquito bites.
5. Mosquitos bite people in order to draw blood. There might be a difference on how mosquito repellent works for people with different blood types. Plus the more data you have, the better you can support your ideas.

Answer Key

Day 4

1. That the type of water impacts how quickly it freezes into solid ice cubes. More specifically, you believe that filtered water freezes faster than tap water.
2. Answers will vary.
3. Type of water.
4. Time it takes for the water to freeze into solid ice cubes.
5. The amount of water placed in each ice cube tray, the temperature of the freezer, the type of ice cubes tray, etc. You might also want to put all the ice cube trays in at the same time so that they all start to freeze at the same time - easier to keep track of data this way.

Day 5

1. Tap water can have dissolved minerals and salts in it - this makes the freezing point a higher temperature for tap water.
2. Different ice cube trays might have different dimensions. This would impact the freezing rate. A really flat and shallow ice cube tray would freeze faster than one that is not as shallow. If you have different ice cube trays, you are changing more than one variable at a time.
3. Water type does not impact freezing time.
4. If you have more than one trial, you have more data to support your idea/ hypothesis.
5. Answers will vary. If you make frozen food, such as popsicles, it might be important to know the different freezing times for different water so you can manage production.

Answer Key

Week 19

Day 1

1. D
2. D
3. C

Day 2

1. Qualitative
2. You would expect to see more females mating with males more often. You could count the number of pairings with one fur color over another. You could also count the number of offspring female rabbits have with male mates of one color fur versus another color fur.
3. Changes in allergy symptoms, specifically sneezing. Number of sneezes (quantitative) or forcefulness of sneezing (qualitative) are two different types of data you could record.
4. You would expect to see less sneezes or milder sneezing (less forceful).
5. Answers will vary. Some ideas include how long they spend around a certain color light or how close they get to a particular color of light. Both of these are quantitative forms of data.
6. Answers will vary.

Day 3

1. Brown fur
2. You would want to know if the male rabbits are similar in all other ways. If, for example, male rabbits with brown fur are also bigger or more protective, then females might have a preference for them but for a different reason than just fur color.
3. That the medicine does not just affect just people with allergies.
4. Answers will vary. The time of day this experiment is being conducted, the placement of the lights, etc.
5. Red light.

Answer Key

Day 4

1. Chickadees
2. Canadian geese
3. Candian geese
4. The cardinal population increased.
5. It increased slightly.
6. 82 Canadian geese

Day 5

1. The table because you were given a definite number - on the bar graph you need to estimate.
2. Quantitative
3. If she is compiling how many times she sees a bird of the same species each day, she might be reporting the same bird over and over. The actual population counts are probably lower than she is reporting.
4. In the winter the population is lowest. It might mean that not many of them survive the winter or, more likely,that they migrate to a different habitat. This second theory is supported by the fact that their population increases quickly in the spring months.
5. The chickadees. Their population number does not shift very much except in March.
6. Answers will vary. In general people can compare the bars in the bar graph more easily. It is a preference however.

Answer Key

Week 20

Day 1

1. D
2. C
3. A

Day 2

1. Number of people shopping in his store at a given time.
2. That time does not have an affect on when shoppers are at his store.
3. How the increase in locust populations is affecting agricultural land.
4. Increases in locust populations are harmful to agricultural land.
5. The sole - a new synthetic rubber was used instead of vulcanized rubber.

Day 3

1. He might accidentally eliminate hours when customers are in fact shopping at his store.
2. If he only has data for one day, he might change his hours due to a difference that only affects one day and isn't a pattern.
3. Answers will vary. Creating pesticides or pest-resistant crops are good examples of solutions.
4. You would want to collect data to make sure an improvement did not occur and then come up with a new idea based on that data.
5. It is more expensive to produce.
6. Answers will vary. One idea is to find a rubber that is less expensive to make but as effective at helping runners run faster.

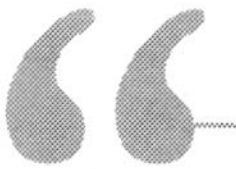

Answer Key

Day 4

1. They used to have to submit their blood sugar levels by spreadsheet once a week to their doctor.
2. The age of the patient is quantitative; the feedback is mostly qualitative.
3. Small size.
4. Patient D
5. The patient and their doctors
6. A smartphone

Day 5

1. Answers will vary. Some issues could be size, data collection, or data management in terms of communicating blood sugar levels with doctors.
2. Benefit: easy to wear under clothing. Drawback: hard to read the monitor.
3. Setting it to read blood sugar levels at different intervals than every 2 hours.
4. Older patients might not be as savvy with smartphones. Also if you do not have a smartphone, or yours breaks, the blood sugar monitor cannot be used. It might be cost prohibitive to some patients who would otherwise want to use it.
5. Answers will vary.
6. Yes, any time a product or an idea is edited, you need to collect more data. You need to ensure that your edits improve what problem you are trying to address.

Made in the USA
Las Vegas, NV
20 October 2021